His
Purpose
My Praise

His
Purpose
My Praise

Relationships, Forgiveness
and Reconciliation

ANGEL M. BARRINO

Angel B. Inspired, Inc.
Charlotte, North Carolina

His Purpose, My Praise

Relationships, Forgiveness and Reconciliation

5th Anniversary Resived Edition

Copyright © 2010

ANGEL M. BARRINO

Revised: December 2010, January 2011, January 2015

ISBN: 978-0-9861335-1-0

For Information Contact:
Angel B. Inspired Inc.
Angel M. Barrino
Charlotte, North Carolina
angelbinspired@gmail.com

Contributions by Michael Ancrum
Cover & interior design by Juanita Dix • www.designjd.net
Author photo by Timothy Wilkins

Printed in United States of America
by Create Space

Father God

Your Word is immutable, Your Spirit undeniable and
Your Love immeasurable. It is because You live that
I truly face each tomorrow. I cannot do anything without You
and I know that I would not have been able to complete
this project if it had not been for Your Grace and Mercy.
Thank you for seeing the very BEST in me.
Without Your spirit living in me to correct me,
I would be reprobate;
without your Word to guide and teach me I would be lost
and without your love to comfort me I would be
in a continuous state of despair. You are my Lord and my Savior,
my Rock and my Shelter . . .
To You I give the glory and honor forever, AMEN!

TABLE OF CONTENTS

SPECIAL DEDICATIONS

This Book is dedicated in honor of my paternal grandparents
Paul and Louise Miller Sr. whose commitment to one another
was severed in death after 50 years of marriage.
I appreciate the example they gave me and the
legacy they left to the Miller family.

For My Aunt Puddin, Uncle Steve, Aunt Clementine, Uncle Zeke,
Cousins Jermaine and Todd, Uncle Gaither, Aunt Ella Mae and
Aunt Daisy on behalf of The Miller Family This Book Is Also
Dedicated to You – We Love you and Miss You!
The precious time you were with us in this life will never
be forgotten, and your memories are always with us.

◆ For My Beautiful Daughter Janae:

You are a gem, a precious gift from God. He blessed me with you
and declared favor over your life from my womb. I pray that you will
embrace who He has created you to be. He has shown me many times
that we will work together in ministry. Often times I know you thought
mommy didn't love you and that I was not there for you emotionally. I
am so sorry for not always being there to help you deal with the pres-
sures of childhood and the emotional issues you faced after your father
and I divorced. I assure you that it is because of you that I write this
book. It is because of the visions God has given me concerning your
life that I have committed to sharing my testimony with others so that
they will not make the same mistakes. It is because of the moments you
comforted me when I was hurting over situations that I thought impossible to endure that I lift my head in victory. It is because of you and the
love you have for me that I submit my life to God once more to be used

by Him to share His love and His Word through song and any other means necessary so that He can be glorified by my life. It is because of you and Him that I now embrace my purpose and ministry to help a dying world know that Jesus loves them. I love you always!

◆ For My Contributor and brother, Michael Ancrum:

Thank you so much for your contributions to this endeavor. Through all of my tears, my frustration, my anger, my disappointment, my laughter and my stubbornness – you stuck by me like a good mentor does and gave me valuable lessons that helped me through this process. I am eternally grateful for your teachings and prayers. Thank you to your beautiful QUEEN Elizabeth for allowing you to help me get this work accomplished. I wanted to list you as the co-author but you didn't actually write anything (LOL) yet you have made such an impact on my life and this book. You have been a mentor and like a father to me. I know many times people questioned your presence in my life but I know that God sent you to help rescue me from myself. I was an emotional wreck when you began to minister to me about my broken marriage. There were many times I did not want to listen, I did not want to follow instructions and I just wanted to do things my way but you still remained true to God's purpose to help me learn what I needed to learn. This book would not be possible without your inspiration and your knowledge of God's Word that you so graciously imparted to me. Thank you so much and your work will never go unrewarded.

*"Praise the Lord! For it is good to
sing praises to our God; for it is pleasant,
and praise is beautiful."*
—Psalm 147:1

ACKNOWLEDGEMENTS

◆ To Joseph Wayne Barrino:

Thank you for all that we endured. The experience as your wife taught me what it means to truly forgive and move forward. I will always pray for you and encourage you to continue seeking God as you pursue your dreams.

◆ To My Parents Ronnie Miller and Katherine Miller:

Without your willingness and love coming together 39 years ago, I would not be here but God used you to bring forth my being into the earth realm for such a time as this. Thank you always for your love and support. I know many times we did not see eye to eye, you did not always accept my choices but you still supported me financially, spiritually and emotionally as much as you were capable of doing. I praise God for you raising me to love Him and to appreciate the gift and love of family.

◆ To My Sisters (Danielle and Karen) and Brothers (Ronnie Jr., J Pass, Chris &LaShanda Smith):

Although we have had disputes and disagreements, I would not have made it through many days without your love and friendship. You are an important part of my foundation – thanks for the tears, laughter and joy you have brought to my life. I love you so much!

◆ To Angela, Tish and Tonya:

The three of you have been my lifelong "sisters", prayer partners and best friends for as long as I can remember. I am a much better person having you in my life. You are friends forever and so special to me, more than words will ever express! Love you eternally.

◆ To My Niece Aerial and My Nephews Joshua and Christian:

You are God's little Angels and you mean so much to me. You have been siblings to Janae and godchildren to me. I love you unconditionally and just know that "Auntie Angel" will always be there for you.

◆ To Samantha Phillips, Sabrina Jones, Sheila Suber, Sharon Braxton, Carla Holman:

You are ladies of integrity, character, spiritual depth and insight, prayer, selflessness and pure fun. I love you and I am so grateful for our sister friendship that have been renewed and established. Thank you for the special place you hold in my heart and for your continual support of my endeavors.

◆ To Rhonda Nails, Katherine Waddell, Tanisha Layne, Laticia Nicole, Anissa Barbee, Rae Jenkins, Liz Bryant, Dawniel Winningham, Tami Wright, Stephanie Wilson, Sally Meadows, Desiree Bonner, and Emelia Adjei:

Thank you for your friendship, partnership and support. You have each been such a blessing to my work and the revitalization of His Purpose, My Praise. I am eternally grateful for each of you and look forward to growing more in business and life with you.

◆ In Loving Memory of Apostle Wanda Love:

A woman who embraced me from the moment we met. Thoughts of her will always be in my heart and mind and I rededicate this project to the world on her behalf. She was a blessing to the rebirth of this book and my heart greatly misses her.

◆ To Bishop Allan Chafins:

Words will NEVER be enough to express the gratitude I have towards you. Thank you for your growing friendship and the business relationship we have established through SIBN. On behalf of The Praise Network family, thank you for being a tremendous blessing.

◆ To The Praise Network Family and Friends:

Without your support The Praise Network would be nothing. Thank you to each and every one of you for the impact you make and the love you show daily to me and this network. (((Hugs)))

◆ To My Other Family and Friends:

My grandma Della, and my **ENTIRE** Miller and Gilmer Families – I love each of you so much! You have been vital to my life in so many ways. I wish I could list your names all right here (Too many to name) but if you know that you have prayed for me, encouraged me, let me cry on your shoulder or anything remotely close then you know that you are special to me. Thank you for always being there. Each of you know the contributions you have made in my life: A special thank you goes to Bettie Sharpe and Beulah Sharpe for your love and for always being there and being supportive; Helen Mitchener, Helen Mahoney, Chandra Graves, Nataisha Pointzes, Lawana Best, Lashonda Stockton, Marlis McAdoo, Shantell Sims, Jacqueline Brannon, Bonita Moore, Purpose and Praise Ministries, The Judah Experience ministry team, Sisters Encouraging Sisters, TEAM Push, Dreams Woven, Wealthy Sisters Network and countless others who have been very supportive in my life and endeavors. To all of my social media supporters and friends who share with me daily by sharing inspiration and supporting my posts – I truly appreciate and pray for each of you. May the blessings of God overtake you!

◆ To Professor Victor Archibong:

You have been my friend, my mentor and like a father. You have believed in me, taught me, encouraged me, allowed me to vent, and you have helped me in so many ways to become a stronger student and "teacher" of life experiences. I thank you so much for seeing the best in me!

◆ To Tara Alexander:

Girl you are funny and inspiring. Thank you for your support and caring. It means so much.

◆ To my Herbalife family:

Moises Sanchez and Vicky Marquez, Rafael Rodriguez and all other Herbalife family thank you for everything you do each day to support others and change the nutrition habits of the world one person at a time.

◆ Pastor Danny Purcell and First Lady Zalonda Purcell:

Thank you! I love you and I pray that God continues to flourish in your ministry. Your ministry is growing by leaps and bounds. To God be the glory.

◆ To Jeff Adams:

You are the best and I thank you for your support and for being a good friend to me, thank you for believing in me and for recognizing God's gift in me and for being a musical genius. Love ya!

◆ To Pastor Michael Thomas:

Thank you so much for your teachings and your obedience to God as He continues to use you as a vessel to bring discipline, correction, encouragement and inspiration to the lives of your members and many people around the world. You cannot know how much your humble spirit and simple, yet profound messages have been a blessing to me and others. Thank you again.

◆ To Dr. John Chacha:

You have no idea who I am, but your teachings and sound wisdom, revelations of God's spirit, dependency on Him and your contributions to The City of Hope in Tanzania have made a significant impact on my life and I have mentioned some of them in this book.

◆ To Mother Theresa Greene:

Thank you so much for being a real woman of God, one who is transparent yet loving and caring. You cannot know how much your spirit and wisdom has impacted me from the moment we met two years ago. Thank you so much for all that you have done to support me and counsel me during this season of my life and your support to this book.

FOREWORD

Each one of us has obtained God given purpose in and for our lives. There is a reason for our existence. It doesn't matter as much how you arrive on this planet called earth, the fact is you are here, and you have to do something with the time you have here.

Unfortunately for many of us we have confused our purpose by inappropriately using in the world the gifts, talents, and abilities God has given us and the outcome is not what we were deceived into thinking it would be.

Being that our purpose is God given we must go to Him in order to get knowledge and understanding of this purpose. It's called the will of God for our lives. He not only gives us the understanding of our purpose but he also gives us the "how to" concerning our purpose. In other words He gives us a complete understanding of what our purpose is and a workable (applicable) knowledge with it. This is called the wisdom of God.

Even so in relationships we must seek God for meaning and purpose there also. It is in this place, where our lack of consistently seeking Him for all our needs that we begin to encounter problems in our life, relationships, or what have you. Well, in His word the plan is laid out, the how to manual is laid out for us, there's really no need for trial and error when dating or when considering marriage, we can just consistently follow this plan of God for our lives and by doing so we can obtain the promises and blessing of God that bring the peace and tranquility we so desire to have.

So what if we didn't do it right the first time? This we must know and understand, God can heal anything, anybody no matter who or what it is. How you might ask? By faith and belief in Him. Our trusting Him in simple obedience to do a work in and through us will bring us to a place of blessings unimaginable.

This book "His Purpose, My Praise" is a testimony written by a chosen yet broken vessel of God, not chosen according to the standards of the world. Perfect by no means! A finished product no! But a humble Woman of God, humbled by life's circumstances. A woman who in spite of her issues she sought and received healing that only God could give. Through many mistakes and bad decisions she has come to and has allowed Him to heal her, so that she can go and share this healing with those whom God will send her way.

Brother Michael Ancrum

INTRODUCTION

The information I am about to disclose to you is the truth and it is my testimony as of date. I have not arrived and I cannot share with you a success story about a marriage that has survived the test of time but I do believe that if I had followed the truth of God's Word I would be able to share that story with you. The simplicity of what I offer to you is to live according to the Word of God and follow His statutes as outlined in Psalm 119. I have purposely kept the chapters easy to read and comprehend. There is no need for me to give you insignificant philosophical jargon as this book is based upon one foundational truth, and that is the truth of God's Word.

God is more interested in our process than He is our arrival. When the Lord makes a promise to us He does not disclose all of the details as to how we are to obtain that promise. We must stand by faith and walk forward to go through the process He has selected for us. Every person's process is different but God's Word is unchanging. In your process, you may have to go through various stages of brokenness, healing and restoration. In your process you may breeze through to the promise of God because you choose to remain obedient to His will which is His Word. Whatever your process is, trust God and follow His path of righteousness for the reward He has released over your life.

Consequently, the spirit of manipulation is alive and well in the Body of Christ and there has been much written about this destructive spirit. Satan desires to destroy men and women of God by tearing down their character and integrity. The enemy uses individuals who are weak minded to propagate his agenda and keep God's children under bondage if they fail to recognize his devices.

With strong intentions, the enemy has unleashed a demonic attack by using manipulation and rebellion to destroy God's most precious earthly relationship. My goal is to expose and destroy the plot of the enemy by revealing the truth of God's Word and shedding light on how the enemy seeks to destroy God's children. No weapon formed against us shall prosper and every tongue that rises in judgment shall be condemned.

Satan accuses God's children and does everything he can to keep us from walking in holiness, righteousness and peace especially when we interact with others of the opposite sex hence the importance of focusing upon the truth of God's Word when preparing for dating and marriage. Satan plays upon people who do not know who they are in Christ, men who do not have a vision, women who are not looking for a vision and people who pursue less than what God truly has for them. Additionally, satan uses distractions according to worldly standards to entrap believers to "connect" with those who do not accept Jesus Christ as Lord and Savior. For this reason, Paul says do not be unequally yoked with unbelievers.

This book also focuses on the importance of holiness before and after you marry. My pastor often teaches that the purpose of dating is to collect data for marriage so unless you are in the preparation stages for marriage you should not be dating. The world's view of dating is much different and completely contrary to the Word of God. For this reason, many relationships and marriages are based on improper foundation and subject to crumble.

Holiness is a process of sanctification which only God can complete within a person. The process of sanctification begins with the mindset of pleasing God and living righteously before Him. When we accept Jesus Christ as Lord and Savior, He immediately renews our spirits but our minds must be transformed from the sinful nature to the new nature which is within Christ Jesus and this can only be done by reading and meditating upon His Word. Joshua Chapter one states, "This book of the law shall not depart from your mouth but you must meditate on it day and night to do what it says to do (paraphrased)."

Before the children of Israel could cross the Jordan River they had to change their old ways of thinking. Joshua said, "Sanctify yourselves, for tomorrow the Lord will do wonders among you, Joshua 3:5." In order for us as Christians to receive the full promise of God we must be set apart. We cannot pattern our lives after the world's way of doing things because we will receive the world's results. Proverbs 14:12 reads, "There is a way that seems right to a man, but its end is the way of death."

As you read, please understand that I am not an expert regarding holiness or sanctification because I have made some foolish choices which compromised my godly relationship many times. I have since realized the importance of maintaining a level of righteousness and peace with God which enables me to come before Him boldly and petition Him concerning my circumstances. Sin separates us from fellowshipping and communing with Him, but repentance brings us back into alignment with Him and enables us to go beyond the veil of Christ. 2 Corinthians 7:10 reads, "For godly sorrow produces repentance leading to salvation, not to be regretted; but the sorrow of the world produces death."

What I present to you are life experiences and practical lessons that I have learned through two marriages and many relationships in my search for love and companionship. I have made numerous mistakes and I have been the victim of someone's selfish desires and choices.

Despite all, the Word of God declares that all things work together for the good of them who love Him and who are the called according to His purpose. So what does this really mean to us? It means that if we belong to Him, no matter what poor choices we make He will turn them around for our good BUT we need to learn the lesson in making the poor choice and deal with any related consequences effectively according to His Word.

Perfecting in Christ is achieving a level of maturity that only comes by being tried in the fire of His furnace. Unless an element is exposed to heat you will not see its true properties or how it will react when heat is applied. Whatever is inside of us, whether we still have worldly attributes or Godly attributes, will come out of us when exposed to heat. Either we will melt under the pressure or we will become stronger and unchanged by the flame. God's plan is designed to make us the best we can be. He wants us to receive all the riches of His glory, all of the blessings He has in store but we must be obedient, we must not waver in our faith and we must be able to withstand fiery circumstances.

Since we have an advocate with the Father through His precious son Jesus Christ we are able to go through our challenges and come out of them victoriously. Until we learn His lessons of obedience, God will continue to allow circumstances to prevail in our lives which prove to teach us what He desires us to learn. God's process is to "tear down, destroy and rebuild" as my mentor Michael Ancrum so eloquently teaches.

This book was written during one of the lowest points of my life. Writing it was difficult because choosing to take the high road and not disparage my current husband was not an easy choice to make. He is a high profile individual and we had a high profile marriage in many aspects. He hurt me deeply, there were things that occurred in our marriage that were unspeakable and caused me a lot of bitterness and pain. There was a lot of verbal, emotional and mental abuse. There were times of infidelity on his part while we were together, there were moments he isolated me and told people horrible things about me, there were moments when I wanted to hate him, there were moments when he neglected me intimately, there were times when he maliciously betrayed me and assassinated my character. There were moments while we lived together that I wanted to do the same things to him that he had done to me; yet I remained faithful to him through those times. God kept me and I endured as much as I could until I could no longer do so. I went to others for counsel and help but was turned away so I began to sink into a deeper hole and a very lonely place. I just wanted someone to hear me.

During the latter season of our separation, I met someone and I developed a close bond with that person but I should not have because I was not capable of another relationship at that time. My heart was hurting, I was broken, confused, destitute, financially and spiritually inept, I was lonely and wanted companionship and I received it though I know it was not God's best for my life. I just wanted someone in my life that was not cruel or hostile; someone who would really love me for me and not tear me down every single day. I wanted someone who saw the best in me, who saw my gifts and abilities and who could help usher me into the presence of the Lord. Blinded by my pain, I started the same cycle that I so desperately wanted to prevent but the turmoil I endured with my husband pushed me right into the enemy's camp and I began a downward spiral straight to darkness once again.

Through my writing, hearing God's Word and His voice come from countless directions; I have made my way back to Him. I had been distracted but God...I had given up but God...I had turned away, but God...He has restored me and welcomed me back into His arms.

In spite of my frailties and failures, despite my bad choices and mistakes, my sin, my shame, my humiliation and public scrutiny, God has given me another opportunity to praise Him, to lift Him up and to serve Him.

This book is evidence of that praise; although it is not a completion it is a stepping stone for more of His glory to be revealed in my life. In this season, I had to be broken. God cannot use any portion of the world in His kingdom, therefore everything inside of me that is not like Him had to be destroyed and is daily being destroyed. I thank Him for His correction, rebuke and chastisement because I know that a loving Father chastens those whom He loves.

This book is not intended to rehash any painful memory of my experience rather encourage you to believe God even when your spouse does not do the same. This book is intended to help someone see that even when it doesn't seem like things are working in your favor, God is still able and He will deliver and protect you from the hand of the enemy.

I pray that you as the reader will be blessed by my words and experiences. In His Service.

A.M. Barrino

"It is not good that man should be alone;
I will make him a helper comparable to him."
—Genesis 2:18

Chapter 1

IN THE BEGINNING

Marriage is designed to be a beautiful relationship if we acknowledge God's sovereignty and purpose for marriage. Often times we choose to marry based on all the wrong reasons. For women, we marry if our biological clocks are ticking, if we want children, we don't want to be lonely etc. Men marry for various reasons as well.

As Christian women and men, we need to seek God's wisdom when choosing a mate. Genesis clearly shows how God brought the woman to the man. He put Adam to sleep when he skillfully designed Eve and presented her to him. He created them to multiply, be fruitful and to replenish the earth; additionally, God created man and woman to cultivate and birth vision into the earth. God brought Eve to assist Adam in

1

the vision God had placed inside of him and her gifts and abilities were "perfect" just for Adam.

Proverbs 18:22 states a man who finds a wife finds a good thing and obtains favor from the Lord. God gives man the ability to choose his mate according to what He designs man's purpose to be. When a godly woman is presented to a godly man both should be equipped with everything needed in order to bring the man's vision to pass. God does not desire for us to be alone in this life and He has ordained marriage for our pleasure but moreover it is designed to fulfill His will in the earth realm. Pull up a seat, take hold and get ready to see your life change as God reveals, through this book, practical measures to make better relationship choices.

Let me address the ladies, since my sisters are very dear to my heart. All the books have been written, *The Rules*, *Secrets of an Irresistible Woman* and others to teach women how to handle themselves with the opposite sex. So there is no need for me to reinvent the wheel. Reading those materials will help you gain a deeper understanding of your position and power as a woman. This book is primarily written for women who need to hear a real life testimony; women who need encouragement but may not be ready to tell their own stories and face the realities of their bad choices. In the process, I want all women to know and understand the power God designed them to have if they submit to Him.

No person upon this earth can teach you the way God can. If you want to know about yourself and you want to know how to relate to another person all you have to do is ask Him. God gives us teachers, pastors, ministers and counselors as leadership to help guide us into the truth of His Word but ultimately the greatest teacher is the Holy Spirit. He guides us into ALL truth and He will not leave us ignorant if we ask Him. The key is overcoming our own selfish desires and moving in line with His Word so that we can ask Him. We do not know what to ask for in prayer, therefore, according to Romans 8:26, the Spirit makes intercession for us.

God being the author and finisher of our faith is concerned about everything that concerns us. Philippians 4:6-7 reads, "Be anxious for nothing, but in everything by prayer and supplication, with thanksgiving, let your requests be made known to God; and the peace of God, which surpasses all understanding, will guard your hearts and minds through Christ Jesus. Additionally, 1 Peter 5:6-7 reads, "Therefore humble yourselves under the mighty hand of God, that He may exalt you in due time, casting all your care upon Him, for He cares for you." Abba Father wants to be the center of every decision we make in our lives; particularly choices we make concerning marriage and relationships.

We cannot be entangled with just anything or anyone and expect that we will receive the fullness of what He has for us. Even though God does give man the ability to choose His wife, He admonishes man to make wise decisions and base them upon His timing and the woman has the responsibility of seeking God to be sure the man who approaches her is one who is fully committed to the will of God for his life and who fits into the purpose God designed for her.

A husband is supposed to cover and protect his wife according to God's Holy Word. Paul proclaims in 1 Corinthians 11 that the head of Christ is God and the head of every man is Christ and the head of every woman is man. The husband should not expose her frailties and faults, her secrets or weaknesses. A true man of God will not uncover his wife but will keep her covered in prayer and protect her spiritually, physically and mentally.

A wife cannot truly be a wife to her husband until she is first a helpmeet. Excluding her capacity to assist him with his written vision, she should be able to fulfill her God given ability to be a helper to her husband or the marriage will not work. God created woman to be a help-meet and suitable for the man to help bring his God given purpose and vision to pass. Anything outside of that is less than God's best for both of them. And He created her to be a wife, to make the home environment more pleasant and peaceful. She was designed to bring balance to the life of the man.

In order to receive God's promise we must be submitted to His authority and headship; if we are not then we should not expect that we will receive anything of Him because we would be considered double-minded. The bible says that a double-minded man (or woman) is unstable and who wants to be with an unstable person. After realizing all that God has allowed me to experience in my life I neither want to be with an unstable person or be wavering any longer in my thoughts or actions.

Marriage is what you make it and not one sided. It takes both individuals along with God almighty to make it work. God must be the center and He must be the head of man, and if the man and woman are both submitted to God and to each other as the Word declares then they can have the type of marriage God has purposed the believer to experience.

The marital relationship is not a trial and error situation. There is no such thing as a "trial" marriage. This is one of the most absurd statements I have heard believers make. Someone even made this comment in reference to my most recent marriage. No one can expect to have quality results if the quality time and effort is not contributed to making a marriage work. God gave us the tools necessary through His Word and equipped the believer with everything that pertains to life and godliness in order to make our marriages function properly.

There will be good times and bad, that is why the vows indicate "for better or worse." Every day will not be a good day but a godly couple takes God's Word and applies it to their situations, prays diligently

4

and they come into agreement with God and each other for the purpose of bringing glory to the master. Consequently, every day should not be a bad day either.

If God be for us, He is more than the world against us so a believer is able to overcome any obstacle and trial; especially in their marriage if both parties are submitted to the Lord.

"But we have this treasure in earthen vessels,
that the excellence of the power
may be God and not of us."
—2 Corinthians 4:7

✀ *Chapter 2* ✀

MY STORY – GOD'S HIDDEN TREASURE

When God began to deal with me concerning HIS idea for Godly marriage I had been divorced from my first husband for almost two years and God had me to read Proverbs 31:10-31. Additionally, He sent women of God who had endured in their marriages, women who had been divorced, and those who had never been married to teach me many valuable life lessons that I had not learned as I developed into womanhood.

The Holy Spirit led me to many conferences and as a result I read many books and devotionals addressed to single and married women. When I began writing this book, I gathered my bible, my notes, journals, and all of the marriage preparation books and videos I had occurred since I began this journey in an effort to evaluate all of the things God had spoken to my heart and spirit concerning the subject of holy matrimony.

Being only eighteen years old when I married the first time, I was immature, afraid and unsure about my identity and I often felt lonely and insecure. Rebellion against my parents was the motivating factor to get married and I was reckless and inconsiderate. My decisions were not based on biblical foundation and because of my insecurities I found myself separated and in divorce court within three years which led to a host of other problems in my life.

Going from one relationship or friendship to another searching for peace, I found none. Searching for love in all the wrong places my best friends had become hurt, bitterness, anger and despondency. Focus on God and His righteousness was not my primary concern and I lacked self-esteem. Although I was intelligent, beautiful and zealous I found myself attracting the wrong people into my life. At the age of twelve, I had given my life to Christ but along the way I fell many times. Born into an emotionally unstable home and being the grandchild of alcoholism, I had become wayward and detached from reality and in my early twenties found myself in a downward spiral. I was headed to hell and self-destruction.

David says in Psalm 139, "O Lord you have searched me and known me. You know my sitting down and my rising up; You understand my thought afar off . . . Where can I go from Your Spirit? Or where can I flee from Your presence? If I ascend into heaven, You are there; If I make my bed in hell, behold, You are there. . ."

As a backslidden individual, I was tossed to and fro with every wind of doctrine. I knew God was my source, my supply and my strength yet was not walking in His victory. Having read Psalm 139 over and over again, one day I cried out for God to rescue me from myself. Although I had knowledge of the Father, I lacked true understanding and discipline of how to apply His Word to my life. The process of God is what I did not truly comprehend and I found myself "kicking against the goads." I would read His Word and sing His praises at church. I would lead solos and sing upon request at other churches but I still lacked true unshakeable faith and a solid relationship with the Lord.

Please understand my disclosure of this information is not meant to disparage me or anyone in my family. My family has been instrumental in shaping my core values, restoring me in times of despair and supporting me when capability affords them to. I merely share this testimony to help you understand the road I have traveled which has brought me to the place in God where I am today.

Desiring love and giving what I thought was love I often times gave my heart to the wrong people. Over and over again, friends would say, "Angel, you do not have to buy love. Just be yourself." I would be confused because I thought that I was being myself but being me meant finding the God in me and being the woman He wanted me to be.

Not long after my first husband and I divorced we remarried. People laugh at me when I tell this part of the story but it is so true. We remarried within months of getting divorced. I even laugh myself because it was such a waste of time and money to go through the process. I truly desired my family to come back together and I lay before God asking forgiveness and repenting for not working on my marriage. Once again, I became actively involved in church and grew tremendously but was still missing something because I wanted a deeper revelation of God's Word and application to my life.

Since I had given my life back to Christ things began to turn around and God truly blessed me in every area of my life yet the marriage still did not seem to work. My desire was for my husband and me to worship together with our daughter but he would not attend church with us on a regular basis. You see, I was not sure about his relationship with Christ and many times questioned him as to why he would not attend church with us. Not to mention I did not realize he had not truly forgiven me for the mistakes I had made.

Being a babe in Christ, I did not know enough about God's truth concerning marriage to speak the word over him and did not find out until later that an unsaved spouse is sanctified through the believing spouse so I began to give up on our marriage again. Honestly, I did not know what to do but still trusted God to do something on my behalf.

One day a good friend from work invited me to attend a bible study class with her. This particular bible study was only for women and was a year long study. When I walked into the church that night I was amazed at how many women were there. Sitting in the sanctuary there were approximately 500 women from all walks of life, all nationalities, races and creeds.

There is power in prayer and there is power in the prayers of more than one person but with all of these women coming together from different backgrounds to pray and study God's Word, can you imagine how heavy the spirit of God was in that place? It was amazing and the Spirit of God never departed from that fellowship.

Jesus, in Matthew 16:17, said to Peter, ". . . And I also say to you that you are Peter, and on this rock I will build my church, and the gates of Hell shall not prevail against it." Jesus is the solid rock and foundation for everything we need in our lives and if we build our relationship with Him upon solid rock, the rock of salvation and truth, who is Jesus the chief cornerstone, then we can overcome any obstacle that comes our way.

If we set our affections upon Him and not earthly relationships; in my case failed love relationships based on worldly standards, then we do not have to worry about being disappointed or heart broken. Even though I was married, I still did not have my complete trust in God because I focused more on the marriage than I did on God's will for my life.

Additionally, when another individual makes up their mind about what they want, you cannot change their mind. Only God can help change the thoughts of man and no matter how much you believe, if the person does not want to forgive or change, they will not forgive or change.

As a result, my first marriage ended in bitterness, anger and hatred towards one another. I asked the Lord to help me and I believed for a season but this man simply did not want to work things out. I became rigid and uncaring, insensitive and withdrawn once more because I thought I had done my best but what I did not realize is many people do not have the capacity to forgive and accept your faults. Later I realized that my hurtful actions toward him were the source of his resentment so I accepted responsibility for my actions and asked him for forgiveness.

Today, my daughter's father and I are friends and we have moved on with our lives and harbor no bitterness toward one another.

I became to realize that although I went to church every Sunday and went to bible study, sang in the choir, led praise and worship; I still had not set my affections upon the Lord. My complete trust was not in Him and His plan for my life. I had zeal without knowledge. And I had placed too much emphasis on people and not enough emphasis on God. But how many of you know that God had a plan despite my choices? He said to me one day, "For I know the thoughts that I think toward you, thoughts of peace and not of evil, to give you a future and a hope. Then you will call upon Me and go and pray to Me, and I will listen to you. And you will seek Me and find Me, when you search for Me with your whole heart. I will be found by you and I will bring you back from your captivity."

I heard this scripture in my mind and my spirit almost as if I were hearing it in my ears. The Lord had spoken His promise to me from Jeremiah 29:11-14 and I was astonished.

Now many of you might say why is she speaking so much about relationships as though she has had a successful one? I haven't had

11

a successful Godly relationship because I have gotten in the way of God's plan many times; yet I now know what God is looking for.

Based on worldly standards, I have had a lot of broken and heart wrenching relationships. These relationships were not based on the truth of God's Word but they "successfully" began and ended because God allowed them to. When God has His stamp on your life, I do not care how many times you try to make something work, if it is not meant to be it will not work. He will show you that you are a puzzle piece that does not fit into that other person's life. This ideal may not make sense to a carnal mind; however, allow me to illustrate what happened in my life when I hooked up with the wrong people.

God allowed me to see the gifts and abilities in others and I often mistook my gift as the green light to enter into a relationship with a person when God only wanted to use me as an instrument of His love and peace in that person's life in order to draw them closer to Him. Hence, these relationships ended in turmoil, hatred and strife. They were inappropriate relationships which drew my attention away from God. These ungodly alliances formed a bond which made it nearly impossible to break up without "tearing" one another apart. As a result, my heart was broken and the other person did not even know why they hated me so much. The Spirit of God had caused them to turn against me because they were not His best for my life.

God's anointing and Word are so vital in the life of the believer especially when matters of the heart are involved. When a believer links up with a person who is not God's choice for them it is difficult to maintain your relationship with God because the balance of influence tips in favor of the enemy or the spirit of darkness. "A season of righteousness or right living" (doing the right things in the eyesight of God) must take place in order for restoration and wholeness to be complete in the believer's life.

The anointing of God destroys yokes and bondages of all types and can bring one back into alignment with God's will if the individual allows healing to take place. But we have a responsibility to submit ourselves as living sacrifices and allow His anointing to destroy the yokes and remove the burdens in our lives.

The anointing is not a gift or talent, feeling or emotion. It is the supernatural power of God that enables us to live according to His truth and His Word. When people are anointed by God it shows and the world is attracted to His anointing. It is almost like when Jesus was led into the wilderness by the Spirit of God and the enemy immediately came to tempt Him and manipulated God's Word for the purpose of trying to distract Him from fulfilling His purpose of going to the Cross. I knew the anointing of God was on my life I just did not know what to do with it. I did not even understand it so I misappropriated the power and gifts God had placed within me.

The enemy has made numerous attempts to distract me from fulfilling my God designed purpose for many years. You see, he studies us and believe me he studied me very well. He had a trap set for me. He listens to our words to hear if any negative confessions will come from our mouths and he manipulates our words for his personal gain. I did not realize that I was speaking contrary to God's will for my life and causing the enemy to have access to wreak havoc.

The Word of God declares that out of the abundance of your heart the mouth speaks and why we have been admonished in the book of James to bridle our tongues and watch what we say. Our tongues are powerful weapons. Death and life are in the power of them. When we speak death, the prince of the air, satan himself is listening so that he can use those words to turn our circumstances around and cause chaos in our lives. Since we as Christians have the creative and life-changing power of God on the inside of us, we can speak life and angels act on our behalf or we can speak death and give satan permission to steal, kill and destroy our lives. Jesus said, "the thief cometh not but to steal, kill and destroy but I have come that you might have life and have it more abundantly."

Michael Ancrum mentioned to me in passing one day that the devil does things intentionally to keep our God given gifts dormant and utilizes distractions (i.e., premature relationships and marriages) to keep us in bondage and enslaved to sin.

Malachi 3:11 reads, "And I will rebuke the devourer for your sakes, and he shall not destroy the fruits of your ground; neither shall your vine cast her fruit before the time in the field, saith the Lord of Hosts." Now I know this portion of scripture is generally used to instruct us on tithing and giving our best to God; however, I submit to you that if satan keeps our gifts dormant; if he blocks our ability to see what God wants to accomplish in and through us; if he can keep us unfruitful and ineffective in the kingdom of God by keeping us entangled with sin, condemnation, unrighteousness and complacency; if he causes us to prematurely go into a ministry or go preach before God says so or shows us how we can use our gifts to achieve worldly standards of success but make us believe that God is leading us in that direction then he has caused us to get off the road that God really desires for us to travel, thereby, causing us to give less than our best to the Lord of Lords and the King of Kings.

If I had remained on the path the enemy designed for me to follow, you would not be reading this book today. My life has been so filled with turmoil to the degree that one chaotic event after another has occurred and these events were all designed to keep me from progressing in the kingdom of God and were designed to destroy me mentally while also causing me to be completely ineffective.

The purpose God has for my life has not been clearer than it has been over the last two years. I have often heard Myles Munroe state, "If you don't know the purpose of a thing, you will abuse a thing." Even as Christians, we abuse one another because we do not know the purpose of being in each other's lives. Often times it is not our intent to abuse each other, sometimes we practice abusive behavior unknowingly.

14

On June 13, 2008 I entered into a marriage without completely examining my spouse's past and did not allow God to fully guide my decision to marry at that time. While God showed me that my husband has a good heart, he had many unresolved issues, hurt and pain that only God could deal with.

In my efforts to love him I pushed him further away because he was unfamiliar with unconditional love. His view of love was one based on the giving of material possessions so he thought I expected something more of him when I attempted to show him the love God had placed in my heart for him. My intentions were not to hurt him or push him away; however, he could not handle the love God had given me for him and as a result a lot of miscommunication and discord erupted in our relationship.

God can heal any broken situation or repair a marriage if both parties are willing to be used by Him in the reparation process; however, I admonish any man or woman to take their time before entering into a situation with someone who has not dealt with his or her past. This does not mean the person is not for you or that you should not pursue a relationship with the person, it simply means that you may not be ready for marriage and you need to seek wisdom from God's Word allowing the Holy Spirit to lead you while seeking godly counsel. One should proceed with caution and practice patience until God releases you to move forward.

Submissiveness to a mate was not an issue for me at this point and God showed me many areas to focus on. I had factored in myself and my emotions, my responses to my mate, healing my heart and allowing the Holy Spirit to minister to me. During my prayer time, I asked the Lord to teach me how to be a virtuous woman and wife. He led me to the books of Ruth and Esther. He told me to read The Song of Solomon and study Deborah and Hannah. He told me to study the woman caught in adultery and He had me to spend a lot of time following the ministry of Jesus which is a ministry of salvation, healing, restoration and reconciliation.

Had I known all of these things before I married the first time then I could have saved myself so much pain and heartache. God has an order, if we follow His plan our lives will be filled with peace and joy.

My prayers were focused on the Lord showing me how to love and respect my mate, how to honor him and meet his needs. I asked God to place His love inside my heart so that the love I give would not be tainted or corrupted, perverted or misappropriated. Spending a lot of time in the presence of God, I repented over things I had done in my past and allowed God to nurture me and mend my "crooked" places but I failed to factor in the man.

I prayed for a mate yet I did not pray for God to truly heal, deliver and set him free before sending him to me. I did not exhaustively pray for yokes of bondage to be destroyed and I neglected to seek the wisdom of God concerning generational curses and strongholds. While I prayed for myself daily to be molded into a godly woman and to be a loving and nurturing wife, I should have prayed in faith for the man God had for me.

There was no doubt that I loved my husband and I believed God for my marriage. After all what spirit filled woman or man of God does not believe God for his or her marriage? But at the same time, I was so hurt and so disappointed, so fragile but I still beloved God for a miracle. I wanted to see the power of God prevail and turn this situation around. Every time I went to church there was a message about a marriage being healed or coming back together and I would start the process of believing God again.

I am sure my desire to save my marriage shocked some of my family and friends but allow me to share with you that Jesus did not cast people away simply because their behavior was unseemly or undesirable. He simply spoke a Word to heal them. In addition, God needs a willing vessel in the earth realm to accomplish His will. In order for this to happen we must stand in righteousness and believe by faith for that which we have asked God to do for us in our prayer time.

My faith to save my marriage slowly turned into doubt and fear because I began looking at the natural circumstances and took my eyes off of God. The Holy Spirit continually reminded me that either I was going to trust Him or I just needed to walk away. He said it was my choice and I needed to make a decision about what I truly wanted from God and what I wanted to see take place in our lives.

Although God showed me what to look for after being married and divorced once before I should have known better and sought wise counsel before entering into my second marriage. First of all, I entered into a marriage with a high profile individual which caused some issues from the onset but I did not realize the depth of what I was dealing with. Secondly, I should have been more diligent by asking my husband whether or not he was really ready for marriage. Since I ignored the fact that he was hurting deeply over issues in his past, I contributed to a situation that could have been avoided had we taken more time to learn about each other. It was okay that I loved him and I believe God gave me the ability to love him; it was just not okay that I moved too quickly in my decision to accept his proposal and enter into a marriage unadvisedly and without the counsel or blessing of our spiritual leaders.

As we will discuss later the dating process is not constrained by natural time but the time frame should be enough to where adequate data is collected in order to make a quality decision concerning marriage. Additionally, "both" parties should be healed from their past baggage and issues.

I began to reflect on some things and thought about the day I had asked my father what he thought about my dating relationship with my current husband, his response to me then was, "Angel, he has been hurt . . . do not hurt him." This was not a green light to get married but rather a caution light to take a little more time in the data collection process. I moved too quickly and as a result my marriage is seemingly beyond repair.

Failing to "interpret" my father's advice as wise counsel; I suffer extreme and traumatic consequences regarding my decision. The bible declares that children should honor and obey their parents in the Lord. Sisters, beloved women of God, please understand that if you have parents or guardians that are living, you should present your potential mate to them so they can offer their approval or wise counsel before you move forward.

If you are unmarried and your parents are living, biblically speaking, you should still be under the authority of your father's house. If your parents are not living, there should be someone in your life whom you can trust and whom you can submit to before making such a life altering decision. There are many women whose biological fathers are not living; therefore, these women should seek to gain counsel from a pastor, a respected uncle or friend who can provide wisdom concerning her dating process.

Women of today are so liberated that they no longer respect the God given authority that their father's possess. The order of dating has been reversed and so many women are "searching" for men instead of allowing the man to "find" them. If we follow the order God established concerning marital and dating relationships, we would not have so many babies having babies or situations in which women are taking care of men versus the men providing for the women.

My father acknowledged that my husband is a good provider and that he is a good man but he has deep seated wounds that needed to be healed before he was capable of loving me the way God purposed him to do.

My husband needed restoration and only God could provide that for him. I could have helped him through that process by being a good friend to him and continually praying for our relationship; we should have presented our thoughts concerning marriage to our pastor and allowed our leadership to work with us to sort through many of the issues we now endure. In retrospect, I realize that I was not ready either. Blinded by my desire to have a godly marriage, I failed to see that I had not dealt with the "things" that cause me to make decisions which are not in my best interest.

Some emotional issues do not immediately come to the surface when dating, particularly with men, because people always attempt to put their "best foot forward" when they are courting. As women we base our decisions on emotions and feelings. Women tend to say, "But you don't know how he makes me feel. . ."

My pastor teaches that Christians cannot base their decisions on feelings because feelings change. Feelings should never be the basis for any permanent decision we make. Wisdom from God's Word and wise counsel from those He placed in authority over us should be the basis for all decisions we make. Had my husband and I taken more time to "collect data" about each other, each other's family dynamics, past decisions and choices then we may still be in fellowship and covenant today. Who is for certain?

Even in the midst of the hurt and pain we both have endured, I believe my husband has love for me and he knows that I love him as well. Through the prayers of the righteous men and women God has placed in our lives, the Word of God that we both continue to receive and our individual relationships with God I believe that healing will take place in both of our hearts. While reconciliation may not occur, I know that in time we will both be vessels fit for the master's use.

I found out early in my life that if I did not have peace in my relationships that I would be disoriented and would find myself doing things to try and fix the relationship. In so doing, I often made a bigger

19

mess of the situation. During this season of separation from my husband, I have had the opportunity to do some soul searching.

On one of my trips to Atlanta, my mother and I had an opportunity to bond. I asked her if I have always been the type of person who wants to "repair" relationships. She told me that since I was a child, I have tried to fix everything. She said that I would cry if I saw animals that were hurt or dead and I attempted to "nurture" or "fix" them too. When she shared this with me I laughed heartily and was able to see why I must have peaceful relationships with everyone. She told me that I loved people and that I loved to laugh. She said I was one of the happiest children she had known but I was also very outspoken and vocal about many things. Given what she shared, I see how God has desired to teach me discipline and constraint when I talk to people because I have always been so open, often to my detriment.

The last two years have been an opportunity for spiritual growth and brokenness. Brokenness by God is not meant to harm us or destroy us rather it is a process of teaching us humility and complete dependence upon Him. In this process, I have tuned into many of the gifts God has placed within me. One of these gifts is a strong desire to show mercy and compassion towards all people. It pains me deeply to see others hurting and I always want to do what I can to help "deliver" people from their bondages and circumstances.

I would be amiss if I did not speak about the second most important relationship in my life next to my relationship with God and that is the relationship with my daughter. For many years, the relationship with my daughter has been strained, although we are growing closer now. My ungodly choices caused a root of bitterness to rise in her and now I am dealing with the negative consequences. I pray daily for restoration because she accepted Christ when she was five and the enemy has attacked her and she believes she is less than what God designed her to be. When we fail to recognize and deal with the sin in our lives

20

our children have to deal with our poor choices. God has given us children as a blessing and they are a heritage but when we do not live a Godly life before them we do them a great injustice and set them up for failure.

Women who are victims of abuse and failed relationships often pass these iniquities to our children. Ladies, our daughters watch us everyday. If your children, especially daughters, see you in an abusive situation whether verbally, mentally, emotionally, or physically; chances of him or her making good choices concerning relationships will be very few unless he or she decides to do the opposite of what you have done.

Pastor Michael Thomas teaches that a woman who is emotionally unstable "became that way due to something some man did to her." In our society today, more and more of our young women are switching to lesbian lifestyles. There are many reasons for this new phenomenon but my pastor teaches that many times it is because of some negative behavior they have witnessed from a man in their lives.

In my case, my daughter rejected me and blamed me for choices she has made and I truly accept that her decisions are a direct result of me not covering her as I should have in prayer, being distracted by the enemy and allowing her to live with her father when she was younger. Her father is a good dad but I do not believe he was spiritually strong enough at the time to completely cover her as a father should. As a result she walks in complete rebellion to me as her mother and to Jesus Christ as her savior and Lord.

Examining our personal relationships and the "factions" or groups of people that we allow in our lives, is necessary as we begin to trust God for a mate. Choosing a mate based on physical appearance or financial status alone cannot be the only attributes we consider. The mate God allows us to choose must be someone who puts God first and seeks Him with their whole hearts. If the mate we choose puts God first then we most assuredly will know that they will esteem us higher than themselves.

Christian women should be especially mindful of the man we allow to enter our lives because if the wrong one comes we may lose our focus on God. Additionally, if you have children from a previous relationship or marriage, take special caution when introducing someone new to your children. If a man does not take interest in your child, chances are he will work to divide your household. Luke 11:17 indicates that a house divided against itself cannot stand. I quickly found out that some of the men I had met after my daughter's father and I divorced were incapable of accepting my daughter as their own. Although they may have been great guys, they were poor husband choices because they did not accept my daughter. How could I possibly have considered them as a mate? This is a major consideration because many times these situations result in neglect and abuse of the child and a man "or" woman who does not accept your children will eventually not accept you. God is so faithful to show you exactly what you need to see in the heart of a person if you sincerely pray and ask Him to show you.

*"But now having been set free from sin,
and having become slaves of God,
you have your fruit to holiness, and the end,
everlasting life. For the wages of sin is death,
but the gift of God is eternal life
in Christ Jesus our Lord."*
—Romans 6:22-23

Chapter 3

ARE YOU "SINGLE" AND FREE? WHOLENESS AND COMPLETION

L isten people of God, being a "single" Christian does not mean that you are eligible to do everything you want to do. In fact, the world defines singleness in a much different way than God does and often times the definition is very unholy. The world says that if you are single you can be who you want to be, you can go where you want to go, you can date who you want to, you can live with your mate before getting married and that you are in charge of your own destiny.

Most of the world's standard is a deception. Worldly talk show hosts have led many on a path of destruction teaching them to follow their own ideals and live according to the world's standard. I strongly believe the Body of Christ has allowed this to take place because we are not fully operating in the capacity God intended for His people to operate in. Pre-marital sex, adultery, homosexuality and other sexual sins are destructive patterns of behavior in the lives of Christians and these sins can cause a person to be entangled with lust and other perversions that the enemy uses to keep believers distracted and completely oblivious to God's purpose for their lives. Being a slave to some of these behaviors, I am able to tell you what the effects have been in my life and later I examine what some of these harmful effects have been. These sins are introduced by satan and endorsed by the world to keep Christians from truly fulfilling the will of God and operating in His spirit.

Being a Christian means that you should be submitted to God and Christ and your lifestyle should be a reflection of such. The Christian single should seek God's Word for principles concerning marriage and the dating process. Christian men and woman should acknowledge God's sovereignty and authority over his or her life and trust that He provides the principles in His Word so that he or she will truly be successful in every area of life, particularly marriage.

God's principles are designed for peace and stability, protection and order so that we as Christian women and men can be in agreement with Him as He brings to pass all good and perfect things for our lives.

A single Christian woman should not be "dating" any one she wants to or chasing after men. She should be single, whole and complete prior to a man of God finding her. Being single in the sight of God is a representation of being whole. After making this mistake so many times because of iniquity and generational curses, I am able to share the truth of God's Word about how He really feels. My mind knew what was right but once you lend your members to "sin" you find yourself repeating behaviors and cycles that God really wants to destroy in your life so that He can truly use you for His glory.

Mathematicians refer to the number one as being a whole number because it is not a fraction. Likewise, Christians need to be whole and not fragmented before entering into relationships, especially marriage.

Another aspect of "wholeness" is beauty in the sight of the Lord. Beautifying oneself as a woman means taking care of herself mentally, spiritually, physically and by working in the Kingdom vineyard – helping others, taking care of her children if she has any, taking care of her home or personal business matters, walking in the fullness of the Lord and the purpose He designed for her and not going outside of the places where He commands her to go. Wholeness or holiness is a precious gift in the sight of God and He desires for us to be whole and complete, mature and lacking nothing.

As stated, being saved and whole are the first two steps to a healthy, godly relationship or marriage. Being free from the yoke of bondage and capable of moving unhindered in the spirit of God is a blessing. God desires that two "whole" people come together to form a union. This means that both individuals should be free or eligible spiritually, mentally and physically (unbound to another). He does not wish that anyone who is not free in their emotions, past relationships or desires be joined with another person because this will be a recipe for disaster. Emotional baggage is a major avenue that satan uses to allow the spirits of manipulation and rebellion to enter a godly relationship.

Paul in his wisdom stated that he preferred Christians to be unmarried rather than married. His reasoning stems from the fact that married individuals are so concerned about pleasing one another that often times God is not first. Since God designed marriage, however, I stand with Him in agreement that if we follow His rules as a single individual then when or if we enter into the confines of marriage we will remain faithful to God's will for our lives. If we do not adhere to God's rules for governing marriage and family, then an imbalance will occur spiritually and the relationship may begin to fall apart. A house divided cannot stand because the enemy will use everything within his power to try and tear down anything God has put together. Yet we know that we have power over the enemy because God has given us His power and ability to operate freely in His authority within the earth realm.

Before entering into marriage please consider whether you are completely free from sinful desires, selfish motives and impure thoughts. Please consider your relationship with God and ensure He is always first. God is a jealous God and He desires that nothing or "no thing, person, or place" be exalted before Him. When we live for Him, He honors our faithfulness and after we have been tried, He blesses us more than we can think or imagine. Then and only then can He truly place you into the life of another for the ministry of marriage to be fulfilled.

Having the desire to be married is a wonderful thing but it is detrimental to marry when God has not completely healed you or restored you from broken situations in your past. Your partner is not your savior and cannot do what God is supposed to do. It is very unrealistic to expect your husband or wife to meet all of your needs because unrealistic expectations keep us bound emotionally. Husbands and wives should complement each other and have enough similarities and differences to make "one flesh." The wife should be the missing part of the husband or "the rib" that God has provided to protect the heart of the man.

Gain control of negative thoughts and feelings about your mate before these things cause problems. Even if you have been hurt in the past it is unfair to transpose negative feelings or "evil" thoughts toward your new spouse. In addition, do not compare your new spouse to your previous spouse or others you have been in relationships with. Comparing your mate to someone else causes distrust and resentment. Utilize the Holy Spirit to help you overcome all toxic thinking before entering the relationship or marriage because the Holy Spirit was given to us as a guide, a teacher and an advocate to help us overcome any areas of weakness in our lives particularly within our marriages and families.

The Word emphasizes the importance of being completely free from worldly thinking or ungodly expectations before we enter His perfect design of marriage. When we fail to allow His power to heal us, we limit the Lord's ability to work on behalf of our marriages and families and we hinder His continual flow of blessings.

In order to receive the fullness of what God has for us, we must operate within His spiritual principles. Deuteronomy 30:11-15 speaks of blessings and curses and what consequences we face when we do not adhere to God's commandments for our lives. Why not choose life and live according to Ezekiel 18? God takes no pleasure in any of us perishing so just "repent, turn and live."

"Who can find a virtuous wife?
For her worth is far above rubies."
—Proverbs 31:10

✖ *Chapter 4* ✖

ARE YOU READY
FOR MARRIAGE?

S everal years ago The Body of Christ encountered what I refer to as the Boaz movement. Pastors, ministers and teachers all across the United States began teaching about this man named Boaz. At every single's conference, women's conference and marriage conference men and women of the gospel introduced Boaz and women everywhere wanted "their" Boaz. If Boaz were alive today he would probably be signing autographs because he had become so popular in the Christian world during this time. Now I cannot discuss Boaz without first speaking a little about the woman who won his heart, Ruth. Her book, her story is where the testimony of Boaz is found.

The themes of the book of Ruth represent those of loyalty, love, submissiveness, restoration and redemption. One of the principles I want you as the reader to understand here is that when you commit to a person in the sight of God and man, when you profess to care for that person and stand by your vows you also connect yourself to that person's family. Chapter one of Ruth begins in the land of Moab in which a man by the name of Elimelech, his wife Naomi and their two sons, Mahlon and Chilion lived. Elimelech died leaving Naomi to care for their two sons. Mahlon and Chilion took wives in the land of Moab and their names were Orpah and Ruth.

The story continues and the two sons died as well, leaving Naomi alone to care for their wives. Naomi was very loyal to them but she knew that she no longer had anything to offer them. She was without a husband, could not have any more sons so she encouraged each of them to go back home to their mothers and families.

The bible states that the young women lifted up their voices and wept because they did not want to leave Naomi yet still she urged them to go back to their native countries. Now when we examine Orpah's response to Naomi one can see that she loved Naomi because the bible says she kissed her but then the bible says Ruth *clung* to her. There is a significant difference here. Deep in Ruth's heart she did not want to be separated from this woman who had been her "mother" since she married Naomi's son. As a matter of fact, Ruth's words to her are shown in verses 16-17. She said, "Entreat me not to leave you, or to turn back from following after you; for wherever you go, I will go; and wherever you lodge, I will lodge; Your people shall be my people, and your God, my God. Where you die, I will die, and there will I be buried. The Lord do so to me and more also, if anything but death parts you and me." My goodness, when I read those words, I felt the power of God.

Ruth was determined to go wherever Naomi went so Naomi must have been a woman after God's heart. The bible further states that when Naomi saw Ruth's determination she stopped speaking to her. She stopped encouraging her to go home and she took Ruth with her back to Bethlehem.

After reading the first few chapters of this powerful book, I realized how wise Naomi really was and God allowed Naomi's circumstances to lead her and Ruth to the destination where He wanted them to be. God led them right to the place where a man of great wealth lived, who just happened to be the relative of Naomi's deceased husband; his name was Boaz.

Upon further examination of these scriptures, I thought about all of the people who kept saying that the woman did not need to do anything in order for her man of God to find her but that is not true. Ruth 2:2 says, so Ruth the Moabitess said to Naomi, "please let me go to the field, and glean heads of grain after him in whose sight I may find favor." And Naomi's response to her was "go."

Ruth had to get into position to receive the blessing and promise of God which by the way I do not even believe she realized what was about to take place in her life. She had no idea what she was actually "gleaning" for. Boaz inquired about Ruth and it was told to him that she was Naomi's daughter-in-law; he recognized her dedication and hard work but Ruth was probably just looking for a way to earn wages in order to help provide for she and Naomi.

After watching her closely Boaz, put her in charge over the other reapers and gave her special privileges. Watch this, he even told her that he commanded the men not to touch her. Wow, let's stop right here for a minute. Ruth had found favor in the eyes of Boaz and she did not even know why. The bible says she fell on her face and she asked him why he had found favor in her because she was a foreigner. Boaz told her that he knew who she was and it was told to him all that she had done for Naomi.

People of God, look how quickly God had turned things around for Ruth when she decided to commit to Him and heed the advice of her mother in law. She had a heart for the things of God and did not even know it. She was humble and she had a quiet spirit, which are worth much value in the kingdom of God *and* to a godly man seeking a wife. The story continues and Naomi gave Ruth instructions on how to handle herself in the presence of this man who was well respected and those instructions led Ruth right into the house of Boaz who redeemed her and took her as his wife.

Ruth's simple acts of obedience to her mother in law, her loyalty, her humble spirit, her willingness to work, her determination, long suffering and patience led her to the promise of God and because she was a willing vessel, God not only blessed her but blessed Naomi also. This story also led me to question why so many women wanted a Boaz but were not willing to take the necessary measures to prepare themselves to receive a Boaz. I remember hearing many of my charismatic friends say they were waiting on Boaz and to this day they are still waiting on Boaz, so either Ruth was already prepared to receive Boaz or the timeline of her preparation is much longer than what the bible indicates. We would have to examine the number of days it took for Naomi and Ruth to leave Moab and return to Bethlehem to get an accurate time frame of how long it took for Ruth to receive the blessing of God on her life. If I might warn you ladies stop talking so much and just start gleaning in the right field.

My experience over the last two years has helped me realize that I either was not gleaning in the right field or I did not spend enough time preparing myself to be the woman God wanted me to be. In retrospect, I realize I should have patiently waited on God and remained obedient to that *still small voice of His Holy Spirit* living inside of me and warning me to be still. Had I listened to Him more closely, I could have avoided so much pain and suffering in my life.

How does God select a mate for us? I submit to you that God does not come down off His throne and handpick our mates. He aids in the selection process by allowing us to know ourselves in correlation with His Word and He allows us to select a mate based on our purpose and destiny. He knows where we should be and He knows where our mate is and He equips the individual to be what we need them to be.

Eve was the first woman and she was pulled from Adam's side but since sin entered God has given man the ability to choose a wife according to what he needs for ministry and companionship. God has not pulled another woman from a man's rib since the beginning. He gives man the ability to select his help-meet that is why the scripture says, "When a man findeth a wife he findeth a good thing." Women should be very clear on this because women should not be searching for a mate, we should not be seeking to find a husband, we should be working for the kingdom of God and doing what He wants for us to do and then God will send the man He wants to redeem us. This man will be one who can cover us spiritually, mentally and physically. This is what Ruth did. She worked and did what she was instructed to do and found favor in the eyes of Boaz. She had godly character and the preparations Naomi gave her led her into the arms of a man of God who understood her worth. When women of God are busy working for the Lord, as the virtuous wife in Proverbs 31, we are sure to find favor in the sight of God and "Boaz."

Each day God shows me through His Word, His vessels and people He has assigned to my life how He is preparing me to be a woman after His own heart. I thought that by my husband "choosing" me and saying that the Lord gave Him favor by "choosing" me that he was truly the one for me. I was so blind-sided because I could not really see that God wanted me to wait a little while longer. Our marriage has been so strained at this point that only a miracle from God can repair it. We have both done things to hurt one another because we did not take the time to communicate effectively or learn each other before we married.

In our separation process, the enemy has played upon our words to keep us in bondage and keep us devouring one another. When I retaliated against my husband's decisions, I made matters worse; as a result, I have become a victim of my own hurt and pain because I did not remain obedient to God's Word.

Proverbs 15:1 declares, "A soft answer turns away wrath, but a harsh word stirs up anger." In response to the enemy, I spoke harshly and I told too many Christian people my situation thus the enemy has twisted my words and used them against me many times. Can you imagine feeling condemned and constantly tormented over a simple mistake as talking too much? God tells us in His Word to watch what we say and control our tongues.

In my efforts to regain the favor of my husband, I shared my heart with the wrong person and circumstances were misconstrued causing further strain and confusion in my marriage. I desperately wanted my marriage to work; I did not want to be a statistic, especially in the church. I was rejected by members of leadership within my church when I went to them for counsel because I did not receive counsel before we got married. All I wanted was for someone to hear my side of the story, hear my heart and help me get my marriage back together.

The enemy used my desire and manipulated the situation for his personal gain and so much chaos erupted in my life and the lives of many around me. The most valuable lesson I have learned from this experience is to go to God first and if He releases you to speak with someone about your circumstances be sure to ask for His guidance regarding who the person should actually be.

Women who are separated from their husbands should be very cautious of who they share information with. The enemy wants to use anything he can to discredit believers no matter what the circumstances are. Even if your spouse does wrong or does not do as the Word instructs; the right thing to do is continue to obey God and listen to Him only concerning your situation. Satan desires to sift all of God's children and keep them ineffective in the kingdom so he will use anything he can to get us off track, even those who say they are our friends.

It cannot be emphasized enough and I realize I have mentioned it several times throughout this book, choose carefully those with whom you share your heart with. You may be an open individual and assume that people are on your side but many are not. People love to talk about things that are "interesting." They love to gossip and repeat what they hear. But God is not pleased with this behavior either; however, He realizes the failures of His "creation." The Word of God tells us to not be tale-bearers and He considers gossiping a sin just like He considers lust and other ungodly behaviors as sin. There is no difference in His eyes and The Body of Christ or those who say they are Christians need to understand His heart concerning ALL sin, not just "sexual" sins or "lust" and pride.

God is so merciful to forgive us of our sins if we only ask Him. We can immediately receive restoration if we go to Him humbly in prayer and seek His face, turn from our wicked ways and acknowledge Him in everything we do. I love the book of Psalms and Proverbs because these books are full of wisdom and guidelines for righteous living.

When a child of God stumbles, as we often do, and our hearts are open to the instruction of God He will "suddenly" bring us back into His will. A simple issue of mishandling situations can throw us out of God's will. For example look at Proverbs 15:10 which reads, "Harsh discipline is for him who forsakes the way, and he who hates correction will die." Not realizing I had condemned myself and held up the flow of blessing in my life by talking to the wrong people and openly exposing many of the events that had occurred in my home, I hurt my reputation and caused shame to be brought upon myself and others.

I felt so alone and empty. I felt worthless and so consumed with guilt after these things occurred because I should have taken everything to God in prayer and stayed quiet before Him. Can you imagine how I felt? I felt like Miriam did after she had rebelled against Moses and God struck her with leprosy as a punishment for her disobedience. She was cast away and isolated until she repented and God restored her. I held my head in shame for months. I could not forgive myself and I had become so isolated and bitter as a result of my own actions. I was truly a woman scorned. My emotions controlled me instead of me controlling them and I had difficulty bringing "my feelings" under subjection to God's perfect will. I had fallen prey to the enemy when he told me that I needed to justify myself and be heard and tell my testimony. In so doing, I made the power of God in my life null and void. At that point, God could not act on my behalf because I failed to operate in His righteousness and peace. He stepped back and allowed me to do my "own thing" until I had made a complete mess of my entire life. Because I was frustrated with myself and thought so many people were angry with me, I isolated myself from the church. However, I am so grateful that I am a child of God and He truly loves me. He disciplined me, rebuked me and restored me. He spoke to me one morning and said, "Do you fear them or fear me?" "Get up and go to church, forgive yourself and sin no more."

Women of God please understand the power that you hold within you. Our hearts are generally so fragile that we do not guard them according to what God would have us do. We allow the enemy to trick us by focusing on the world's way of handling situations instead of allowing God to fight our battles. When we do this, we change the atmosphere around us to one of bitterness and negativity. No one wants to be around a contentious and bitter woman, even if she is justified and speaking truth concerning her situation. The bible declares that it is better to be on a roof top than to dwell with a contentious woman.

Women have the wherewithal to affect their entire environment either for good or evil. Focus on Hannah for a moment. In the book of Samuel 1:8-18, Hannah went to God before Eli the priest and prayed for a son. The bible says of her in verse 13, "Now Hannah spoke in her heart; only her lips moved, but her voice was not heard." Hannah prayed out of the abundance of her heart, sorrow and grief because she desired to give birth to a son. She confused the enemy because she did not speak out loud but from her spirit and God answered her prayer. Do you see how much power she held within herself to take her sorrow and grief to God and allow Him to change her circumstance? You and I have this same power if we will use it and present our petitions before God instead of before man and the counsel of the ungodly.

Years ago when I prayed to God for a godly mate, I asked Him very specific things. I desired a mate who loved God more than he would love me because surely if he loved God more than he loved me he would know how to love me. I prayed for many other things that I will not disclose because they seem so trivial now but the point is I sought

God for the type of man I desired to have in my life. I did not care so much about all of the physical things although I did pray for a mate that would be pleasing to my eye and whom I knew that I could dwell with through good and bad times and work with closely in ministry.

During that time frame, just before I met my current husband, the Holy Spirit spoke to me early one Tuesday morning and said, "your husband is not who you expect Him to be." This message came a long time after I had prayed my initial prayer for godly companionship. I had no idea what to do with that information; I did not know the time frame for which God was bringing this man to find me. I was so clueless about this and was not aware that the enemy may have actually heard the pronouncement God had made in my life as well and he would send many "Ishmaels" into my life.

I dismissed the prophetic word the Holy Spirit spoke to me and filed it away in my mind until I met my husband. Surely this was God (is what I said in my mind) but I honestly did not fully seek God on how to proceed and now I truly understand the importance of seeking counsel and asking the right questions before making a decision to marry. Once we were married I asked God's forgiveness in moving too quickly, even though my husband and I connected, I was not aware of all of the emotional scars he had suffered.

I believe God forgave us both and I trusted Him to guide us in our walk together and believed God for everything concerning my husband's life. Yet my husband and I were not on the same page. Maintaining a marriage is hard work and unless both parties work together it will not survive. I believe that if we had worked together, God would have honored our marriage and restored our relationship but there were so many people in the middle of our situation that it was nearly impossible for either one of us to stay focused on the will of God.

Much of what I share in these pages is reflective evaluation after these events have passed. I realize I made a mistake, I realize I did not spend enough time getting to know my husband, I realize all of the things I did wrong now but while I was in the middle of it, I did not want to hear everyone's negative opinions. I did not want to hear that the marriage was potentially over. I did want to hear that we got married too soon. I just did not want to hear any of that at the time I was going through it because I still believed God could work a miracle.

Emotional baggage from either partner will destroy a potentially healthy marriage and may cause division and strife making it nearly impossible for you to reconciliation. Marriage must be nurtured and cared for (as any living organism must be) intently with the Word of God and His presence at the very core of the relationship. Ecclesiastes 4:9-12 reads, "Two are better than one, because they have a good reward for their labor; for if they fall, one will lift up his companion, but woe to him who is alone when he falls, for he has no one to help him up. Again, if two lie down together, they will keep warm; but how can one be warm alone? Though one may be overpowered by another, two can withstand him. And a threefold cord is not quickly broken."

Consider this, at the center of a marriage is the Holy Spirit of God to lead us and guide us in our decisions, establish our household and help us stay strong in the midst of marital challenges. He becomes part of that three fold cord in our marriages. He is the glue that holds everything together as my pastor often states. If both partners are filled with God's spirit, what can the enemy do to them or their marriage? What can adversities and challenges do unless we allow them to overtake us and deteriorate the bond God is strengthening?

Marriage is a covenant and since God honors covenant between two believers, He is obligated by His Word, the Word that we speak back to Him to help us build our marriages and families. If we step outside of His Word then we step outside of His will and we open ourselves and our marriages to the attacks of the enemy. Satan does not need much to destroy a household. He only needs an area of darkness that we allow to exist in order to tear apart something that God truly desires to grow and sustain. God needs healthy marriages and families to help fulfill His will in the earth. Darkness in the lives of believers opens the gateway to hell and all of its evil forces into the earth realm and we will find ourselves fighting against "principalities and the rulers of darkness" in the form of our loved ones.

So many people are looking for solutions to life's problems and the Body of Christ holds the answers with the Word of God yet we have more problems than people who do not acknowledge Him as Lord and Savior. Statistically, the divorce rate in the church is higher than those who are not saved and profess to be Christians. How can this be? What are we doing people of God and why are we not allowing our Lord to help us live triumphantly in every area of our lives? Why do we not deal with the human condition and our worldly state of mind before we attempt to enter into such life changing circumstances? We should have strong marriages and healthy families and we have more brokenness, despair and sin in the church than there is in the world. I can speak of it because I have lived it.

Divorce should not be an option in the household of God. Yet we as Christians turn quicker to divorce than the world does. We look for the easy way out because we do not want to give up our way of doing things. We do not see marriage as ministry and the design God has chosen for His people in order to show the world a better way to live. We accept any and everything into our lives and expect God to bless us and give us more but we do not want to make the choices He has outlined in His Word.

Preparation for a godly marriage begins at the beginning, middle and end of His Word. Whether we realize it or not, sexual sin is one of the most powerful and destructive sins known to man. When we engage in premarital or extramarital sex a powerful thing occurs in the spirit realm and most people do not even realize what actually takes place. Sex is not only a physical act it is a joining together of two people, a man and a woman, in the spirit.

When believers engage in sex with someone God has not approved for us, the spirits of lust and perversion present themselves and the act

41

becomes one that grieves God's spirit and God is holy and cannot look upon sin. He turns away from us at that moment and we wonder why condemnation and guilt immediately appear.

When we repent and turn from such destructive behavior God can act on our behalf. If we continue to practice such sin as believers we will find ourselves completely out of the will of God and doing things that are contrary to His purpose for our lives. God cannot look upon sin because He abhors it. Remember when Jesus was crucified and darkness fell upon the earth the darkness represented God turning His face from His only son. Jesus was without sin yet became sin for us that we might live life eternal; therefore, God could not look upon His only begotten Son, even though He loved Him so much. Since Jesus bore all of the sins of the world within His body on the cross God had to turn His head until Jesus proclaimed, "*It is finished.*"

In a marriage, when the two become one flesh, God looks upon the sexual relationship and honors it, blesses it and calls it good. His spirit is still present to join the man to his wife and God blesses the fruit of their bodies and causes righteousness to overcome any area of strife in their lives. The marriage itself represents union to God and the sexual relationship represents communion with Him. Can you see why God said sex must be saved for marriage? However, many married couples find themselves in a situation where they feel guilty for desiring their husbands or wives or they do not see consummation of marriage or coming together physically as holy; but God says the marriage bed is undefiled and He instructs husbands and wives to make sure they practice physical intimacy on a regular basis for the sole purpose of keeping the enemy out of their marriages so they will not engage in temptation or infidelity. In fact the only time God says that husbands and wives should not be intimate is when they are fasting and praying. In all things, husbands and wives should be in agreement and this includes physical intimacy. Additionally, God designed sexual intimacy for our pleasure in marriage and for the purpose of reproducing children if the couple desires to have children.

Satan attacks this area of a marital relationship because he realizes how much power exists between a man and woman if they are joined together sexually. His plot is to destroy any "seed" or fruit that is produced in a godly marriage. In this case the seed can be children or any vision that is produced out of a godly marriage. As I stated in Chapter one, a woman must be able to help meet her husband's vision.

For example, my husband's vision was to start a record label. When he shared his vision with me, my spiritual womb immediately begin to position itself to help birth into the earth realm what God had promised him in the spirit realm. This is part of the purpose of a help-meet; to help your husband bring to fruition that which God has placed inside of him. When a man gives his "seed" in this case my husband's vision because we do not have any children together, the woman receives it and produces fruit or a baby, in my case helping to bring to pass that which God had placed inside of the man I had made my vows to.

God showed me this revelation several years prior while I was still in the preparation stage for being a help-meet. The knowledge and wisdom God has placed within my spirit concerning marriage and divorce enables me to understand that I have been chosen to help a man of God be successful in this life; however, the process is not easy especially when you fall into areas of failure.

Queen Esther was presented to King Ahasuerus *after* his wife Queen Vashti betrayed him and was dethroned. Esther was brought in along with other young virgins and remained in the preparation stage to become queen for one year.

The bible says in Chapter 2 of Esther, "Let beautiful young virgins be sought for the king; and let the king appoint officers in all the provinces of the kingdom, that they may gather all the beautiful young virgins to Shushan the citadel, into the women's quarters, under the custody of Hegai the king's eunuch, custodian of the women. And let beauty preparations be given them." Esther was not presented to the king before her time and she spent numerous days being groomed and "molded" for the task.

First of all, Esther was of Jewish descent and was not supposed to be Queen but God had a plan. The word of the Lord continues saying, "In Shushan the citadel there was a certain Jew whose name was Mordecai the son of Jair the son of Shimei, the son of Kish, a Benjamite . . . and Mordecai had brought up Hadassah, that is, Esther, his uncle's daughter, for she had neither father nor mother. The young woman was lovely and beautiful.

When her father and mother died, Mordecai took her as his own daughter . . . and when many young women were gathered at Shushan the citadel, under the custody of Hegai that Esther also was taken to the king's palace, into the care of Hegai the custodian of the women. Now the young woman pleased him, and she obtained his favor; so he readily gave beauty preparations to her, besides her allowance. Then seven choice maidservants were provided for her from the king's palace, and he moved her and her maidservants to the best place in the house of the women." Wow, this young woman was so stunningly beautiful that she obtained favor from the first time Hegai laid eyes on her. Yet she still went through the preparation process before being presented to the king.

God had chosen her to be queen and she prepared herself for the completion of that selection process by going through the customary twelve months of preparation. For six months she used myrrh on her body and for the next six months she used perfumes and other preparations that were used in biblical times for the purpose of beautifying women.

Okay ladies, she was already beautiful but she had a little bit more that God wanted to do in her life so He placed her in the preparation process and as the story continues she became Queen and had much favor in the sight of the king and with God. What a powerful testimony and it only took God one year to complete the process because Esther was already lined up with the will of God for her life. As a result, God used her as conduit to bless His children and help deliver them from bondage.

I asked God if I were ready to be married at the time I entered into this second marriage and I see that I did not stand complete in my faith for my marriage to work. My past and present relationships with family and friends spilled over into my relationship with my husband. As I look back on my actions I see that I did not always speak my husband's love languages and in turn pushed him away. He felt that I was too affectionate but I thought affection is what he desired. Even though I do not agree that there is such a thing as a person being too affectionate, I accept how he felt. I was not obsessive and in my mind there is a clear distinction between affection and obsession. I thought I had done everything right. I thought I was being an excellent wife but he was still unhappy. No matter what I did for him, it was not enough.

I knew that God was able to change His heart, but I did not remain steadfast and unmovable, abounding in the work of the Lord. I should have kept praying and believing, continually petitioning God for deliverance and restoration. I should have asked God to show me what my husband needed from our marriage and should have communicated a little better with my husband concerning his needs and desires.

Even though I fell short in some areas, I still did all that I could to make a peaceful home and love my husband unconditionally. I did everything I knew to do with what God had placed inside of me concerning being a godly wife. I was not perfect but daily sought to please God and my husband and be what he needed in order to fulfill his God given purpose. I loved him past his faults and failures and supported him wholeheartedly for every endeavor he pursued. I wanted to be who God desired for me to be and I tried ministering to my husband's needs on a daily basis while continuing to build our home and contribute as he needed me to do. My efforts all seem in vain because despite my attempts to bring our marriage back together my husband proceeded to maintain our separation. Many times he mentioned reconciliation but then he would retract and pull away and we have maintained separate lives for more than a year.

"And the vessel that he made of clay was marred in the hand of the potter, so he made it again into another vessel, as it seemed good to the potter to make."
—Jeremiah 18:4

Chapter 5

FROM MESS
TO MINISTRY

Remember in Chapter two, I indicated that relationships are important to me however I really did not know how to function in relationships in my younger years. I read in a devotional that the rifts in our relationships are a direct reflection of our relationship with God.

God loves us so intently and esteems us greater than the angels. We have been created in His image and likeness according to Genesis 1:26. Since we are created in His image we should desire to be more like Him. God's Word teaches us to seek His will for our lives. Throughout scripture we see the importance of conforming our minds and hearts to the blueprint God has laid out for us in His uncompromised Word because His love for us is designed to protect us from hurtful situations.

Paul one of the greatest authors and ministers who walked the face of the earth left us with so much encouragement in the New Testament that we have no excuse for not living life the way God intended. Paul admonished us to be content and be strong in the Lord. He urged us to seek God's face and be adamant about our walk with God so that others could see the light of Jesus in our lives.

We should be content in our relationships, our purpose and our lives so much so that the enemy cannot distract us, yet many times we are not content because we continue to do things our own way. This contentment should stem from perpetual peace in God and contentment in Him regardless of what occurs in our lives.

Romans 12:1-2 states, "I beseech you therefore, brethren, by the mercies of God, that you present your bodies a living sacrifice, holy, acceptable to God which is your reasonable service. And do not be conformed to this world, but be transformed by the renewing of your mind, that you may prove what is that good and acceptable and perfect will of God." This is a very familiar passage of scripture and is often quoted in our churches and in conversation with other believers yet many of us are not living to this standard that God has given us.

We make choices everyday. God set before us life and death, blessings and curses and advised us to choose life. If we continue to walk in our carnal thinking we walk in death. If we walk in the promises of God, the simple rules that He set before us then we walk in peace and life. Walking in peace means living life so inwardly calm and still in His presence that peace, love, joy, patience, goodness, mercy, and self control exude from our inner being; walking in peace means standing still in the face of adversity and allowing God to fight on your behalf.

Walking in peace means that when everything and everybody is testing your patience you can speak a word from your spirit and command the waves in your life to be still. How was Jesus able to sleep in the midst of a storm while the disciples were all filled with anxiety? He was filled with peace. He spent time with His Father in heaven so much before His earthly ministry began that the peace of God ruled His life. He was not moved by the storm tossed waves of the sea and He stood flat footed before those waves in the face of the disciples and spoke that which was inside of Him, peace. God has given us this same power.

We can command the mountains in our lives to move and the storms inside of us to be still. Going through this ordeal with my husband, God used a few people to help orchestrate peace in my life. His Words spoken through others was for me to "stand still and be quiet." He told me to keep my mouth shut and at first I struggled because I love to communicate openly about things that concern me. I love to be around people and I wanted to make my point and let everyone know how justified I was and how righteous I was. What a fool I was being because I was keeping God from being able to work on my behalf.

The true test of my righteousness came when I began to shut up and watch God move. He began to calm the storm inside of me then the noticeable changes around me took place. I stopped talking as much. He moved me from a place of distortion and anxiety to a place of rest. Everything around you can be falling apart at the seams. The enemy will try to tell you that you are going to lose your mind. People around you will be going crazy but God will hide you so deep in Him that the enemy cannot find you. His rest is a place of not only peace but also one of joy. And for a season I maintained this peace but I guess I became too comfortable and let my guard down. There is nothing like the rest of God.

You may feel like your world is falling apart but the promises of God are still yes and amen. He will comfort you in the midst of your trials and tribulations because He promises to take care of His children. As I write these words, I am still in the healing process and still learning God's way of righteousness and obedience but daily being transformed in the renewing of my mind.

Constantly blaming my husband, God told me to look at myself. He told me to walk in His will and He would handle everything else. The life lesson here is that if you are married and you and your husband are experiencing difficulties or the realities of separation and divorce have set in, again please be careful who you talk to and what you share with them. Out of frustration and hurt, many women tend to discuss their feelings openly with the intentions of sorting through the emotions and that is where I found myself but everyone is not at a spiritual level where they can handle your situation.

When you share too much of your situation with the wrong people, they formulate opinions, gossip and cause much more confusion than necessary. Again this is where dependence upon God is so vital. God wanted me to lean completely on Him. Proverbs 3:5-6 states, "Trust in the Lord with all your heart and lean not on your own understanding; in all your ways acknowledge Him, and He will direct your paths." Well how could God direct my path if I were not leaning on Him to begin with?

I called friends to ask them what they thought and the Holy Spirit would say, "Ask God what He thinks." What a powerful yet simple revelation. I noticed how people did not want to talk to me anymore because who wants to talk to a bitter wife? And as I reflect on those days of seeking someone to talk to about what appeared to be the end of my marriage, I realize that I would not have wanted to talk to me either. Sometimes I laugh about it now because God stood there waiting on me to turn to Him and in my stubbornness and my own volition, I kept running into a brick wall.

The truth remains however that I am deeply hurt over everything that has occurred and angry with myself for not doing things the right way. I wanted to see a miracle happen in my marriage despite what others thought. Jesus told Paul that he was kicking against the goads when Paul persecuted the Christians. I was trying to fix the marriage on one end but tearing it up even more on the other end because I just would not be quiet and listen to the voice of God.

Standing still is the position I needed to maintain because we belong to a very prominent and spirit filled ministry. My husband is well known and our lives had been easily visible due to his status in the music industry. Although he initiated many of the circumstances we endured, it was my responsibility as a servant of God to maintain a level of composure that would not draw more attention to myself and my husband.

My intentions were not to harm his reputation or bring disdain. I merely wanted someone to listen to me and help me through my pain. It is always easy to see your mistakes when you step outside the situation but God is a God of forgiveness and restoration. Although I spoke the truth regarding my situation, my behavior was irresponsible and damaging to say the least.

As a Christian woman whose faith is strong and who knows God's Word immensely, my responses should have been a little more discrete. After I acknowledged my careless speech and confessed my sin God restored me and simply told me to began the process again of being quiet and allowing Him to work. He is the only one who can fix problems and situations that seem impossible to fix.

As I think about the numerous times in my life where I attempted to help God do His job, I realize that things did not change for me until I stepped out of the way. Righteousness is not an easy position to take when you are hurting. Righteousness causes you to step out of your comfort zone but agreement with God and His Word are the first steps to walking uprightly.

The Word of God is like a grape vine. The vine is the life giving source for the fruit. In John 15:1-8 Jesus says, "I am the true vine, and My Father is the vinedresser. Every branch in Me that does not bear fruit He takes away; and every branch that bears fruit He prunes, that it may bear more fruit. You are already clean because of the Word which I have spoken to you. Abide in Me, and I in you. As the branch cannot bear fruit of itself, unless it abides in the vine, neither can you, unless you abide in Me. I am the vine, you are the branches. He who abides in Me and I in him bears much fruit; for without Me you can do nothing. If anyone does not abide in Me, he is cast out as a branch and is withered; and they gather them and throw them into the fire, and they are burned. If you abide in Me, and My words abide in you, you will ask what you desire, and it shall be done for you. By this My Father is glorified that you bear much fruit; so you will be My disciples."

Jesus is our life giving source and He is one with our Father God. Jesus is the Word of God which was manifested in human flesh and He showed us how to walk in agreement with Him, Father God and the Holy Spirit. If we abide in Him and His Word the truth of God abides in us, we can walk in righteousness before God and walk in peace with those in our lives regardless of what events occur.

Nehemiah was a great leader for God and he held fast to his position of rebuilding the walls of Jerusalem as God instructed him to do. The enemies of God wanted Nehemiah to come down off the wall but he told them no and that he was doing the work of the Lord and maintained his position of righteousness before God. He refused to fold and succumb to the devices of the enemy because he knew that if he did not do what the Lord commanded him then the city of Jerusalem would be destroyed. God used Nehemiah mightily and as a godly example of what we as Christians should do when the walls of our own lives are threatened by enemy attack. We need to hold our position and let the enemy know that we are doing a great work and we are not coming down off the wall. After studying the book of Nehemiah again, I realized that I had not been holding my position faithfully and I compromised my position in God by getting involved in foolish things and spending too much time focusing on what the enemy was doing and not enough time focusing on what God was doing.

I had been ministering as praise and worship leader at my church and through the music ministry God began to elevate me past my fears and intimidations but all of this was compromised because I was blind-sided by the enemy. Having ministered in song for years at weddings, programs, and other church services; I never really stepped out into the true call God had for me because of my fears. I have recorded with numerous artists as a background vocalist but still did not understand the importance of my relationship with God truly being built on solid foundation and allowing Him to minister to me before going out to sing unto His glory. I did not realize that my greatest gift to others would be birthed out of great suffering and pain and administered through song and proclamation of His Word. I took for granted the things that God had spoken over my life and allowed the enemy to have too much access into my life. I had stepped out of my purpose, came down off the wall and took my off Jesus and in doing so I began to travel down the road of despondency and isolation once more.

True ministry is about what you can give to others and how you respond in certain situations. I was too focused on myself and not focused enough on the will of God for my life and the lives of those around me. If we take a look at the lives of Jesus, John and Paul neither of these great men of God were moved by circumstances and the tasks ahead of them. I realize that my gift of song is one that God truly placed within me and when I sing, I pray and ask Him to sing through me so that I am removed and He will obtain all glory and honor. At times when my lifestyle was questionable before Him, I could not minister and He began to show me that I must have a pure heart before Him in order to sing because if I did not stand before Him in righteousness my sinful lifestyle would affect those I would minister to.

I was under the impression that part of my ministry would be with my husband by following him in his music ministry and being supportive to him as his wife but I realize that there is much more to music ministry than my gift and talent, my character is important and God is transforming my character into His so that I can truly be effective for His kingdom. I realize that often times in the music industry there are individuals who do not have the character of God and they compromise the Word of God in order to become successful as artists. I did not want to do this, so God dealt with me concerning the issues in my life, my character, integrity and pride until He released me to sing again. Although, I no longer am a praise and worship leader at my church, God is using me in other avenues and I am working on a solo project and ministering as a background vocalist with a local gospel group. In addition, other doors of opportunity to minister have been opened to me and I am so grateful that God gave me another chance to use that which He has given me.

God does not care about a gift or talent if our hearts are truly not toward Him. We can operate in gifts and talents but God is more concerned with faithfulness and what is in our hearts. For example, there are people who may not have the gift of song but they have the character, faithfulness and heart God desires for true ministry and He will use them because of the anointing on their lives. Remember, His anointing destroys yokes and removes burdens; therefore, He can use anyone whose heart is towards Him. Can you imagine how His anointing might fall and how He will move when a person who has been allotted the gift of song, realizes that it is not about them, and their hearts are truly right before Him?

God can change a person's voice and He can give them a gift if they so desire because His Word says in Matthew 25 that He gave more talents to those who were faithful and utilized their gifts and abilities for His good rather than for their own selfish gain. When we truly acknowledge that God can use anyone, despite the strength of their abilities, to perpetuate and bring Glory and Honor to His name then we will have gained the true essence of what ministry is actually about.

*"For whom He foreknew, He also predestined to
be conformed to the image of His Son, that He
might be the firstborn among many brethren.
Moreover whom He predestined, these He also called;
whom He called, these He also justified; and whom
He justified, these He also gloried."*
—Romans 8:29-30

❧ *Chapter 6* ❧

PURPOSE
AND POSITION

So many difficult circumstances have come into my life and at one point I thought I was under a curse because so many chaotic things were happening to me. I began to question God and have made so many efforts to understand why He allows these unfortunate situations because it seems I am under constant persecution. Often times I feel like Jonah because I want to run away from what God is trying to do in my life. I am convinced God has a sense of humor because when I ask Him these questions His response is "begin again child, you are stubborn, hard-headed, you are not in control of this and you are no different than anyone else."

God has chastened me since I accepted Jesus as Lord and Savior. In rebellion and stubbornness I tried to do things my way and God showed me what my prayers had been since I accepted Jesus into my heart. My prayers went something like this, "Lord please make me more like you, crucify my flesh. Mold me into your image and likeness." Well, when you pray a prayer like this please know that your life will not always be easy. I have prayed similar prayers over and over so when persecution came I should not have been surprised but little did I realize that many of my sufferings were correlated with my prayers. Christians should not be surprised when persecution comes because we have the mind of Christ.

Jesus was persecuted, despised and mocked while on Earth and suffered great persecution for the purpose of going to the cross and dying for a sinful world. In Revelation 2:10, Jesus spoke to the persecuted church and said these words: "Do not fear any of those things which you are about to suffer. Indeed, the devil is about to throw some of you into prison, that you may be tested, and you will have tribulation ten days. Be faithful until death, and I will give you the crown of life."

One of my favorite poems is *Mother to Son* written by Langston Hughes. This poem seems to be the theme of my life. He says, "Well, son, I'll tell you: life for me ain't been no crystal stair. It's had tacks in it, and splinters, and boards torn up, and places with no carpet on the floor – bare. . ." My beloved, I submit to you that my life ain't been no crystal stair but God has been molding me and shaping me into the image of His dear son. Why could I not see this before? Why could I not see my purpose until now? Distractions whether big or small, keep us from seeing the direction God leads us in. He continually speaks to us and leads us but we ignore His leading and go away like sheep led to the slaughter.

Allowing the cares of this life, particularly in my marriages and other relationships; the affliction and weight of doubt and uncertainty to engulf me many times, I missed God's attempts to bring me into complete alignment with His Word and His purposes for my life. Even in what seems to be a failed attempt at marriage once more, God teaches me and allows me to see myself.

As I indicated, I wanted to go my own way, wanted to leave the church, wanted to stop singing and subsequently left the minister's class for a season and I almost gave up on God but He said, "No, stand still." He told me that His grace was all I needed despite the things I had done. He beckoned me to trust Him and be quiet. Although I briefly returned to the ministers' training class I was afraid of what my leaders thought about me and my reactions concerning my marriage. However, due to escalating circumstances, I was forced to step down from all ministry functions including praise and worship until God dealt with me concerning some serious issues in my life.

As I think about all of this, I know that I was not prepared for anything that happened since I married this man. Never would have I imagined enduring the things I have gone through over the last few years but when you are out of the will of God turmoil is what you will face. Evidently my process was not complete and I was not ready for marriage because I clearly made some wrong decisions; however, I am so grateful that God uses the traumatic circumstances in our lives to work for our good and cause us to grow and be better. Even though I was in a tough situation, God still protected me.

Wise counsel would have shown the light on much of what I have encountered; however, God is still able to do exceeding, abundantly above all I can think or imagine according to the power that works within me.

Position is not based on locality but based on spiritual condition and mental stability. When my husband and I initially separated, my spiritual position shifted because I began to waver and doubt what God could really do for me in this season. My position should have been one of continual prayer versus listening to the voice of the enemy and not being moved by external circumstances. God used my direct leadership at church to help me make sense of things because my thoughts were so scattered and I was very close to mental breakdown.

In order for God to work through us in times of devastation we must stay vertically aligned with Him and not be moved by what we see or hear. God can only act upon our faith and no matter what, His word should take precedence and be flowing from us in order for Him to move on our behalf.

Purpose is what keeps a child of God moving forward and pressing toward the mark of the high calling which is in Christ Jesus. In this process of pressing toward fulfillment of one's God designed purpose, a flood of "evil forebodings" or negative thoughts, challenges and unimaginable circumstances may come. If we are not rooted and grounded in God's Holy Word, an obstacle will alter the path of God for our lives.

Deacon Ancrum stated to me one day, "As we walk with God in this world God allows us to see the hurt, pains and ills of others. Some of these will attract our attention and hold it. Many times within us is the knowledge that we can and must do something about what God has allowed us to see, usually this is an assignment or purpose. Since we have gifts and talents or rather abilities within us which can satisfy or help eradicate what we see, we should be more earnest in our endeavors to quickly believe God in accepting His will to 'seek and to save.' Passion to do or desire to remove this hurt and pain gives the go and strength to go forth and save, heal, and even deliver them that we see." This message he gave me helped to set me free in spite of my mistakes, my sin, my failures and the loss of my marriage.

My purpose has become clear in that I know God has selected me to be a wife of noble character but He is still trying to remove those things which prove to be toxic in my relationships. He has instilled His character in me which means that as He continuously shapes me into His likeness, He is breaking and tearing down the foolish things I have obtained from the world. My mind is being conformed to be like Christ's which means that when I interact with others now I can respond from God's character and not my own.

Additionally, my purpose is tied to the people God has assigned to my life, the ones who need to hear of His love and forgiveness and His salvation. His purpose for me is knitted in restoration for His children and giving to those who are in less desirable conditions than I have been in.

Even though on the surface my purpose has been clarified, it is much deeper than having a successful godly marriage or successful relationships with my family and friends. His purpose for me is based on pouring into the lives of others that which He has placed within me and seeking and saving those that are lost.

Charity begins at home and then spreads abroad so how can I minister to the lost, the brokenhearted, the despondent and hurting people of this world without first standing in a position of deliverance and restoration with my daughter and in my other relationships? Galatians 6:1-5 reads, "Brethren, if a man is overtaken in any trespass, you who are spiritual restore such a one in a spirit of gentleness, considering yourself lest you also be tempted. Bear one another's burdens, and so fulfill the law of Christ; for if anyone thinks himself to be something, when he is nothing, he deceives himself. But let each one examine his own work, and then he will have rejoicing in himself alone, and not in another. For each one shall bear his own load."

Now how could I possibly restore my daughter or draw her to Christ if I am not healed emotionally? How could I possibly have been a witness to my husband when I reacted to his behavior versus praying and standing still in the midst of adversity? These are simple practices yet profound because my loved ones are watching my lifestyle and watching my reactions while looking to see if I am going to act upon the faith I profess to have or whether I will fall apart when adversity comes.

When God chooses your purpose, He equips you with every gift, talent and skill required to achieve that purpose; therefore, when you seek Him for your purpose and move into a position where He can bring that purpose to fruition consider your family, consider your surroundings and your own spiritual condition. Moving too quickly into your purpose will cause your position in Christ to shift because God cannot bless something that He has not given permission to begin. While He has equipped us and enabled us with everything we need to fulfill our purpose in Him, the choices and decisions we make must line up with that purpose and we must be capable of handling any consequences that follow.

I Corinthians 10:13 says, "No temptation has overtaken you except such as is common to man; but God is faithful, who will not allow you to be tempted beyond what you are able, but with the temptation will also make the way of escape, that you may be able to bear it." How wonderful God is to know how much we can bear; the situations He allows to enter our lives are an indication as to how much He has equipped us with. For example, look at the life of Job.

The bible declares that Job was an upright man and did not sin. God had a hedge of protection around Job so resilient that the enemy had to ask for permission to test him. Job 1:6 says, "Now there was a day when the sons of God came to present themselves before the Lord, and satan also came among them. And the Lord said to satan, 'from where do you come?' So satan answered the Lord and said, 'from going to and fro on the earth, and from walking back and forth on it.' Then the Lord said to satan, 'have you considered my servant Job, that there is none like him on the earth, a blameless and upright man, one who fears God and shuns evil?' So satan answered the Lord and said, 'Does Job fear God for nothing? Have you not made a hedge around him, around his household, and around all that he has on every side? You have blessed the work of his hands, and his possessions have increased in the land. But now, stretch out Your hand and touch all that he has, and he will surely curse You to Your face!' And the Lord said to satan, 'Behold, all that he has is in your power; only do not lay a hand on his person."

God already knew that satan was going to enter into His presence and ask for permission to test someone or "devour" someone so God gave satan permission to test the most righteous man on earth at the time. God knew how much Job loved him and despite the loss of his children, his possessions and nearly his health, Job did not curse God. His own wife told him to just curse God and die but he did not. He had the fortitude to stand in the midst of adversity and because he did, God restored much more to him than he had possessed before.

My pastor often tells the story of how God gave him the vision of our church, Love and Faith Christian Fellowship; however, if he had moved too quickly in building the ministry he would not have been able to handle it thus possibly aborting the true call God had for him. He obeyed God and because of His obedience our ministry reaches millions of people nationally and internationally.

In contrast, when I rebelled against my father and married my daughter's father, I made a huge mess and nearly destroyed my daughter's life in the process because I was not prepared to be a godly wife let alone a mother. Consequently, I moved into a second marriage without being completely emotionally healed and allowed the traumatic events to push me into a place of isolation and despair thus creating a barrier between me and God and what He really wants to accomplish through me. I also failed to consider the emotional turmoil my husband suffered as well. The point I attempt to make here is that when you position yourself to be used by God in any area of your life, if you are not completely free in your emotions you will cause things to shift spiritually. Remember when you accept Christ you are no longer your own, you are dead to the things of the world and your flesh should die as well. Therefore you should not be surprised by any fiery trial you face, as 1 Peter 4:12 states. Count it all joy brethren when you suffer for Christ's sake and take a personal inventory of your state of mind, emotions and other factors before moving into any area of ministry or into any relationships because people pay attention to how you handle sufferings and situations when you name yourself with Christ.

Nonetheless, remember that you as a believer have been purchased with a price, the precious blood of Jesus and His death gives you the freedom to walk away from guilt, shame and any other "evil" that attempts to keep you in captivity. Once you repent and ask Him to forgive you, your life begins brand new and God can and will continue to use for His glory. Never allow people or the enemy to hold your past against you and keep you from walking in peace and fullness with God.

"Then Joshua rose early in the morning; and they set out from Acacia Grove and came to the Jordan, he and all the children of Israel, and lodged there before they crossed over."
—Joshua 3:1

❧ *Chapter 7* ❧

TRANSITIONS

A t the onset of everything, my health began to fail, I started losing my hair, my job was on the line and my mind was all over the place. I had gained nearly 50 lbs. and was pre-diabetic. I could not seem to pull myself together even though close friends and family told me to get my thoughts under control so that I would not lose my mind. At the suggestion of a good friend, I began reading Joyce Meyer's book, "Battlefield of the Mind." When my husband and I separated in August 2009, I enrolled in school full-time and started taking charge over my health by going to a local nutrition club. Although outwardly I seemed to progress, inwardly I still suffered anguish over things that were happening in my life.

Another friend of mine, Pastor Vander D. Purcell, shared some powerful words with me when I asked him what to do when you don't know what to do. He said, "You are in the valley of decision and standing at the Jordan River which represents transition." Those words rang in my mind as I thought about my current circumstances.

I had to make some quick decisions and I had to move myself into a place of peace but I did not know how. I prayed for my marriage and prayed for my daughter's deliverance but I was in the way of what God wanted to accomplish. My will overshadowed His will and I could not seem to let go of the pain despite friends and family telling me, "Angel, let it go and give all of this to God." I had become so stressed out that the only words proceeding from my mouth were, "I have a headache."

Everyday for months, I felt this agonizing pain in my head and left side and all I did was pop pain pills and keep going. I did not realize how sick I was becoming. I missed many classes and my professor reprimanded me and almost gave up on me. My supervisor gave me chance after chance and until she finally stated, "you must do something." So I took some vacation time but it still did not help. I knew where I was headed but I could not make my heart and mind line up with each other. My mind knew that I should set my affections on God but my heart had been torn into a million pieces and I had such a hard time focusing on the will of God for my life. As time went by, I would have good days and bad days until one day things fell apart again and I simply shut down. This is when things really took a turn for the worst. I was physically sick and did not know it and began to lose an astronomical amount of weight. I kept going through this cycle of getting better then getting worse because I was being pulled in so many directions. Promises were being made, promises were broken and this cycle of emotional turmoil continued for months.

At church we sing a song that says, "He reigns forever, He reigns forever, He reigns forever and ever more . . ." but the words of the song did not seem to matter very much to me. I would go to church, sing, listen to the Word then come home and be miserable because I internalized everything. I was so filled with anger that it was hard for me to see God and what He really wanted to do for me.

People of God, do not allow anger and disappointment over failures consume you because then you negate the power of God and you exalt the circumstances rather than exalting God. Jesus proclaims, "If I be lifted up from the earth I will draw all men unto me." How can He draw you closer to Him if you are constantly wallowing in self-pity and condemnation over past mistakes? Pastor John Chacha says, "Your yesterday ended at midnight." I began to practice the words of my direct leadership, my friends who were earnestly praying for me; I began to focus on the teachings of my pastor and many others who admonished me to just let go and let God. There was literally nothing else I could do. I had been allowing the circumstances to control me and if I walk in the spirit of God and I carry His Word within me, there should have been nothing to change my course. God intervened quickly and He started dismantling the flood of negative thoughts that consumed me.

I had a difficult time processing the fact that God forgave me for talking too much about my situation. I had a difficult time processing that God forgave me for moving too quickly into another marriage because I had listened to everyone tell me what a mistake we had made and that God would not honor our marriage, that it was not ordained and God did not put His stamp of approval on it. For weeks I walked around in condemnation and confusion because I allowed myself to be drawn away and enticed by people's interference but I know that God had already made some promises to me concerning my marriage. I accepted my mistake but was still being crucified by it because "everybody" thought they knew of what God really wanted to do in my marriage. Instead they should have been concerned about their own marriages or situations instead of being so critical of mine. God is able to repair any broken situation, in fact He specializes in mending broken places and restoration yet there were very few people who stood in agreement with me concerning my prayers for reconciliation.

I saw the heart of the man I fell in love with. I spent numerous hours, days and minutes praying for him and asking the Lord to bless our marriage and take us to another level spiritually. God showed me that He wanted to use us for His glory but somewhere, somehow we got off track. My faith faltered because I listened to the voice of the enemy rather than listening to the voice of God. Satan would accuse me and say things like, "See you are crazy. You don't know what you're doing; you don't know what you are talking about. God is not going to bless this mess. God will not bring this marriage together because you were intimately involved before getting married. God is not going to bring this together because it is not His will for this marriage to work."

My husband and I made some mistakes in the beginning of our marriage. But my faith was strong enough to say, "Okay God, we messed up. Please forgive us. Please restore us and give us another chance to get this right." From there, every prayer that I offered to God He honored; every situation that my husband and I faced, I petitioned God in prayer and He moved heaven and earth on our behalf. So who can tell me that God does not repair and restore?

I look around at some of the marriages in my church and I look at the marriages of close friends and many of them did not start out in correct alignment with God because they made mistakes, but God has blessed them tremendously and they are vessels that He uses. My mind said," what gives another person the right to decide how God will work concerning a situation?" God can use anyone He wants to use. He used Rahab and she was a prostitute. He used David and he was a murderer and an adulterer. He used a donkey and He used many others who were less than perfect in His sight.

While my husband and I made a mistake, I felt we corrected our mistake by going to God and repenting; we committed our marriage back to the Lord during the first few weeks of being married. Abraham and Sarah got off track by giving birth to Ishmael through a concubine but God still honored their prayers and gave them the precious promise of Isaac. What gives Christians the right to decide what God will do in circumstances? God can turn anything around and bring glory to Himself. He is God and beside Him there is no other.

People told my husband and me that we did not date long enough. This was the last thing I wanted to hear at the time, although as I began to go through the healing process I realized we did not take enough time to get to know one another prior to marrying.

There were ten years between my first marriage and my second yet I still did not have enough information available to me in order to make an informed decision to marry my current husband. Who can put a time frame on how long to date a person? This is one of the questions I kept asking myself but I realize that time was needed to really see the truth. Although God does not have those types of time frames in His Word and the dating process is not constrained by natural time the time frame should be based on an individual's relationship with God and their eligibility, maturity level and wholeness. It is according to our faith and our state of being when we come to Him with our requests. God will show us what we need to know in order to make quality decisions but God's responses are not based on man's natural concept of time.

God is infinite so I kept asking how we can restrain Him to our inception of time. Moses was able to receive within forty days and nights the entire history of the beginning of mankind. So how do we box God into our time constraints and limitations? My husband and I dated for six weeks before we got married but the problem was not necessarily the length of time we dated but rather the state of emotional wholeness prior to meeting one another. Neither of us was emotionally whole and I did not ask enough questions during this process nor did I labor before God long enough to know everything I needed to know in order to determine how much more time we needed to take before making such a dramatic life change.

Covenants are serious and marriage is one of the strongest covenants there is so after we married we had an obligation to God and ourselves to work towards making things right. We made a mistake but that was not a legitimate reason to walk away from the bond we had formed.

Initially I asked God to show me the heart of the man who wanted to marry me and He did. The Lord showed me that my husband was tenderhearted and loving but his spiritual heart was covered up with so much other stuff that layer upon layer of baggage needed to be removed before his heart could truly be seen. These are the things I took to God in prayer and I asked Him to remove those things and God said, "You do what I have required of you and I will honor your marriage." He said, "Leave your husband to me." Months went by and we had good days and bad days. Things would seem to get better for a season and then they would get difficult and I really did not understand what was going on.

I remember one day in April 2009, my husband woke up early and went to the living room to pray which was something I had never seen him do before. I knew some things had been troubling him and I had been praying for His mind to be at peace and for God to give him strength for the things he was facing with his children and other issues. He knelt down and he petitioned the Lord and when he came back to bed he held me and spoke these words, "Baby, the enemy is going to attack you, me and our marriage so we need to stay in bible study and stay in prayer with each other." I looked up toward heaven and whispered, "Thank you Lord."

God had been answering my prayers but little did I know the enemy was about to come in like a flood. The Word says that when he does come in like a flood that the Lord will lift up a standard against him. Shortly thereafter the flood gates of hell opened in our lives. It seemed that all of my prayers and faith went out of the window. I began to grow weary once more and I knew that there were some outside influences causing some of this havoc in our lives. Still I prayed and asked the Lord to intervene but my husband allowed the enemy to come in. Do you see how important it is to stay rooted and grounded in God's word? Faith without works is dead and I am living proof. When he spoke those words to me that morning it was a clue that something was about to happen but I allowed myself to be caught off guard by the things that surfaced. I also allowed the enemy to use me because anger crept in and I began to retaliate.

Women and men of God, if you ever have to deal with a situation such as this, trust God and God only. Do not be conformed to the things of this world but set your affections on Him and trust Him. Even if the marriage did not come back together right away, my faith should have superseded all that was going on around me.

As I stated in previous chapters, people tend to offer their opinions and make judgments based on what they see but at night when it is just you and God, they do not see how you feel. They do not see or hear your cries of suffering or pain nor do they know what you endure or go through to pull yourself together enough to face the world. They whisper behind your back, they gossip and manipulate your words and they crucify you for being human. you feel and just tell you what they think is politically correct. Others might sincerely be there for you but cannot offer the truth of

Regaining your momentum or self-esteem after devastating situations is exasperating yet people will say to you that it should not be if you are a child of God. Rarely do people understand that outward behaviors are symptoms of root problems within a person. People do not misbehave or act unseemly just because they want to; they have good reason in their minds but may not know how to overcome the poor behavior.

Having a person or a few people in your life who are truly capable of ministering to you without offering their opinion is important.

Some friends might negate how God's Word because they do not know enough of His Word to apply to your situation. Others may not have gone through emotional, verbal or any other type of abuse and they run from you because their own problems are too great.

Still some may have experienced what you have or worse yet because they are not healed themselves cannot offer you any consolation based on God's Word because they are bitter and angry also. Pray and seek God for the right person who can help you through the healing process. God sent me some "angels" during this process to truly minister the truth of His Word. They stood with me and comforted me in times of despair and they encouraged me to keep moving forward in the things of God.

When my marriage first began to unravel, I consulted very few people because I really wanted to do things God's way. Closer to the time we separated, I leaned on people that I thought were fully grounded in God's Word but realized they had not been through what I had been through. They did not know what it meant to be in the position I was in so they could not possibly offer me any counsel from God's Word. The only thing they could give me was their opinion and what they thought God desired. As a matter of fact, very few people that I talked to concerning my situation actually prayed with me. They said they were praying for me but they did not pray with me and in my attempt to save my marriage, I isolated myself from those who were actually willing to pray with me and restore me.

My direct leadership was among the few who actually shared the complete truth of God's Word and worked to stabilize me emotionally so that I would not lose my place in God. They prayed many times for emotional healing and only spoke the Word of God to me; they did not tell me what I should or shouldn't do. Only God could do that. There were others who offered the same consolation many times but some of them did not possess the patience required to help me through this process. Currently, I have a few people I trust with my heart and my feelings. Not many are interested in hearing too much more about the traumatic events that have occurred but they are interested in my progression into wholeness and maturity in Christ again.

My actions contributed to a huge mess but I have moved forward with my life and I realize that dwelling in past failures only give the enemy more power over my life. Many people want to see me succeed and overcome the hurt and pain which I have endured.

Day by day, minute by minute, hour by hour I focused on what I could have done to keep my daughter from choosing the lifestyle she has chosen. For weeks, I meditated on what I could have done to fix my marriage or what I did to cause it to end. It ended long before it really had a chance to begin but I refused to face that reality. No one could see the emotional turmoil I continued to go through because of the outward facades they witnessed. Internally I was dying and God had no where to reside because my mind was constantly filled with negative thoughts about my life. After many text messages, emails and phone calls later to friends, family and even my husband, I can truly say that God has given me strength and each day things become easier and better.

Resting in God while in transition from one place to another spiritually can be so difficult because while you are in that place of moving into His rest and peace the enemy will do everything he can to keep you from getting there and staying there. Psalm 91 clearly states, "He who dwells in the secret place of the Most High, shall abide under the shadow of the almighty." I was not dwelling in His secret place, so peace was very far from me. I did not even know how to dwell anymore. Not only that, if you are a person who is accustomed to handling certain situations like I am, you may be inclined to handle all situations the same way; but, some things can only come out by prayer and fasting as Jesus said to his disciples when they attempted to cast a deaf and dumb spirit out of a young boy. They were not equipped to heal this child; they could not fix his situation.

Likewise, I found out during this last year that my hands just cannot fix the situation with my marriage and neither can I fix the situation with my daughter. I am completely insufficient of what is required to fix anyone's situation including my own. My dependency for all of these situations is totally in God.

Struggling for months with my health and my weight, partly because of low self-esteem coupled with stress, depression and anxiety I have had much work to do in order to get my life back on track. Going back and forth to the doctor, I had been diagnosed with having an incurable illness and severe immune dysfunction which caused me to become adversely ill affecting nearly every part of my body for several months; I began to miss so much time from work as a result of the pain and depression I was experiencing. I thought I was dying and because there were so many things hitting me at one time I was ready to take my own life. There were so many times that I thought God had given up on me and was angry with me for the choices I made.

Despite how I felt and how much pain my body was experiencing, I had to present my petitions to God so that healing and deliverance could take place in my life because I still have work to do in His kingdom and I accept the responsibility for which He has given me although I have not arrived. I thank God for my physical and emotional healing everyday and with each passing moment I take some of my power back. I am still growing into His purpose for me and I have learned so much over the last few weeks that I praise Him for keeping me when I know I could be dead or lost once again.

When hopes and dreams seem to be shattered, all seems to be gone, nothing seems to work out the way you planned, lift up your eyes to the hills from which comes your help because your help truly comes from the Lord and your hope should be in Him. Never allow anything or anyone to tell you any differently.

Coming from a place of darkness and feeling like I could not make it, feeling like I was unworthy of love and invaluable to anyone, believing that everything was my fault and seemingly accepting the destruction the enemy wanted to perpetuate in my life I have moved to a place where I accept responsibility for my actions yet I no longer accept condemnation. Accepting condemnation is against the will of God because His Word clearly states that once we repent and accept His forgiveness we are free from guilt and condemnation.

Through the experiences of my past and present God has shown me that He wants to deliver me and my family. He has broken and destroyed generational curses and iniquity yet there are still issues that need to be dealt with and can only be overcome by His Word and continual trusting in His power. I accept His will for my life and I accept whatever the consequences may be based on decisions that I have made. I can truly say, "It is well with my soul."

*"But you are a chosen generation, a royal
priesthood, a holy nation, His own special people,
that you may proclaim the praises of Him,
who called you out of darkness into His marvelous
light; who once were not a people but are now the
people of God, who had not obtained mercy
but now have obtained mercy."*
—1 Peter 2:9-10

❧ *Chapter 8* ❧

REVELATION

I cannot begin to chase down the intricacies of how my marriage failed. At this point all of those factions are irrelevant. The point is now, the situation is in God's hands and I have taken responsibility for the words and actions I contributed to the marriage breaking down. True friends have supported both of us. They have prayed and fasted, they have listened to my side and his side and they have counseled us night and day on what we should consider doing.

As I begin to see myself in this situation, God used a few people to bring out of me that which He had placed in me. This book was placed within me years ago but the experience of my recent marriage along with the support of true Christian friends has given me the courage to write it and present it to women and men who need to hear the truth of God's Word concerning His most precious earthly relationship.

As I have stated throughout these chapters, I shared too much not realizing that I was even doing so; deep hurt and pain will make you do some insensitive things and you may find yourself at a place where you do not even remember what you said or did. Women of God, never do this. If you are going to confide in someone let it be someone who is tested and tried as a true friend or counselor who will keep your confidence.

My husband may have contemplated on restoring the marriage, however, hope for restoration is questionable because of everything that has occurred. Outwardly I seemed untrustworthy. Even though I felt he was untrustworthy and did not have my best interest at heart many times, it was still my responsibility to protect this situation as much as possible. Listen to me women of God, no matter what your husband or mate does, give it to God and be cautious who you talk to. You may think you are receiving wise counsel, you may think you just want to sort things out, but your actions are what people watch when situations like this explode and your mate is watching you as well.

Your husband may say all sorts of things to people but utter not a word and give it to God. If you do not, you will be the one looking unstable and insecure and will have many regrets later. This is a lesson I should have learned many years ago but I realize I am dealing with a seed of iniquity that was passed down from many generations before. When God began to show me myself through His Word, I realized I was still dealing with issues that I thought were completely gone. It took my marriage falling apart to realize those things were still there and God had to deal with them because I cannot enter into the areas of ministry He has called me into with these unresolved issues lingering inside of me. The effects of what my husband and I have done to each other still seem to reside as I write this book but my prayer is that we will have peace.

Someone said to me, "Angel, it is no longer about what your husband has done but now it is about what you can do." She said, "Look at yourself." My godly friends remain true to me and continue to pray for me and my husband daily. There have been many others who have spoken words of encouragement, prayed and fasted, and just believed God for His will to be done.

James 1:15 reads, "Then, when desire has conceived, it gives birth to sin, and sin, when it is full-grown, brings forth death. The death of my marriage began long ago but I spoke too openly and publicly about the situation thereby forsaking the righteousness God wanted me to stand in and caused more harm than good. Remember I said God needs a *willing* vessel in the earth realm to accomplish His purposes. I helped to escalate the extreme conditions for which I have now been subjected to by obviously confiding in a few people who could not truly pray on my behalf.

None of the details really matter, all that matters now is God's perfect will being accomplished. Satan desires that I do not write this information because the light of God's Word always dispels darkness. If satan can prevent the light of God's Word from shining in those hidden areas of our lives woe to the kingdom of God being established for us.

Although I initially ignored the voice of God when He said, "Stand still, I will fight for you," I have since regained my foundation and submitted to His complete authority over my life. Another friend, LaSonja, spoke prophetically to me in the first stages of my despair and said, "God wants to shower you in this season. He wants to love you and He wants to provide for you, rest in Him." Her willingness to be used by God to assist Him in my transition from brokenness to wholeness meant so much to me.

The questionable looks and suspicious stares I have received do not seem to matter as much anymore. I am able to stand firm and move forward in the things of God knowing that the testing of my faith produces patience. An associate pastor at our church admonished me that the greater the trials the greater the ministry within a person. I can see the hand of God not only on my life but on my husband's life and God has given me a glimpse of what He truly desires from His people.

The work of true ministry is never easy but if we submit to God's will and way of doing things, He gives us the grace to handle anything we must endure. The ministry of each person is different, that is why God placed pastors and teacher, prophets, evangelists, apostles and lay persons in His Body. We cannot all function the same but being fitly joined together we must work together to accomplish His perfect will in the earth. His commandment is to go and make disciples of all men, teaching and preaching the gospel and not adding anything to it or taking anything away from it. That is a simple commandment which many of us fail to understand because we have so many other things on our minds thus we attempt to conform God to what we want instead of conforming ourselves to what He wants.

God's mind concerning my life is what I now seek to understand and implement. There are too many souls depending on me; my daughter's spirit and soul hang in the balance so I do not have time to pity myself any longer or dwell on past mistakes. Philippians 2:5 states, "Let this mind be in you which was also in Christ Jesus, who, being in the form of God, did not consider it robbery to be equal with God, but made Himself of no reputation, taking the form of a bond-servant, and coming in the likeness of men."

Another valuable lesson I have gained from my experience is the importance of Christ like humility. If we can remain humble before God; He will exalt us in due season. My desire is to be so much like Christ that everything I do must glorify Him and if it does not then I do not want to do it. I asked the Lord in my prayer time recently, "Father how can you get the glory out of this situation and my life?" His response, "Focus on me and my purpose and I will handle everything else."

David says, "Thy Word is a lamp unto my feet and a light unto my path." God's Word does not return to Him void and it will accomplish that which He sent it to do. He sends His Word to heal, deliver and set free. When I began to trust Him, when I began to meditate on His statutes I gave God credence or authority to work on my behalf once again. Galatians 5:1 reads, "Stand fast therefore in the liberty by which Christ has made us free, and do not be entangled again with a yoke of bondage." Bondage is anything that keeps us from freely worshipping or serving our Creator. The fear of failure and despair, what people thought of me and the feelings of insecurity or despondency held me captive. My mind had become a danger zone and I began to sink into the deepest place of darkness I had ever known. As I write these words, God has rescued me from myself and from the snare of the enemy.

True freedom comes not from knowing about what God can do or that He is God, but from lifting up your eyes and trusting Him while walking in the direction for which He commands you to walk. It comes from being able to acknowledge His sovereignty and see the place for which He desires you to go and bring your acceptable sacrifice. Abraham trusted God when God asked him to sacrifice his only son. The Word says in Genesis 22:3 that he rose early in the morning, saddled his donkey and took two of his young men, the wood for the burnt offering and Isaac his son and went to the place God told him to go; however, for three days he must have agonized over what God wanted him to do because it was on the third day that he lifted up his eyes and saw the place where God wanted him to be. His obedience was better than the sacrifice because God honored his faithfulness and spared Isaac's life. For this reason, God deemed Abraham as a friend and multiplied his seed upon the earth and blessed him to be the "father of many nations."

Even though I really made a mess of things by talking to some of the wrong people and made a few unwise choices concerning my marriage, God has restored me and He is taking care of me. He promises to protect us and keep us as long as we agree quickly with Him and get back in line with His Word. He does not hold our mistakes and sins against us, although people condemn us and do not allow us to get beyond the mistakes of our past. His Word declares that He is faithful and just to forgive us and cleanse us from ALL of our sins if we submit to Him and His will for our lives.

Dr. John Chacha recently spoke at our church and confirmed many things that my pastor and a few spirit filled friends have taught me. He said, "You must face your giants, you cannot run from them." My inward desire to run from all of this kept me from truly moving forward in the spirit of God even though outwardly I seemed okay. My mind had been grappled with mind boggling spirits, as Joyce Meyer teaches. These mind controlling spirits kept me from experiencing true freedom in God. When your mind is stagnant everything around you seems to be irreversible. Dr. Chacha spoke of possibilities and true faith and dreaming and having visions. Until that day I could not even remember the dreams and visions God had given me. Additionally, I did not even think I was capable of ministering or proclaiming the Word God has placed within me. My mind kept saying, "Everyone is looking at you. Everyone is mad at you. You do not have any friends. You are worthless and now you cannot go into ministry because people will laugh at you." What a trick of the enemy. The thoughts he interjected began to take over my mind and God's thoughts of peace toward me were gone.

Nonetheless God spoke through Mr. Ancrum and said, "Write down your visions and dreams." He told me to outline the things God has shown me concerning my family and my daughter. Additionally, I have moved to such a place of contentment within Him that I do not worry so much about my mistakes, I am learning from them instead.

The words my minister of music spoke to me also resonate within me. She said, "You cannot run from what God wants you to do. You still have to move forward and if you do not get off of this emotional roller coaster, everything will drive you crazy." So many others said the same thing. Much to my surprise, I was the only one who could stop the roller coaster. The control that the enemy had over me (through people, my husband, etc), the games, the hidden agendas and manipulation the enemy used to keep me "unraveled" was an illusion that I could end simply by trusting God and speaking His Word over my life.

I was so concerned about what my leadership thought about me. I realize now that the situation may have been too explosive for my pastor or other leadership to get involved. Besides, God wanted to do a work in and through me that He has been trying to do for many years. Additionally, I had to learn that I could not continue to allow what others thought of me to control my ability to function in the kingdom of God.

As God continues to usher me into the place where He desires me to be, I ask Him daily to give me strength to overcome every obstacle and challenge. I ask Him to keep me from pride and arrogance and help me to remain in humility before Him. Even though I am a victor and no longer a victim, I must be mindful of my behavior and actions so that I do not seem to be mocking or walking in pride. In order for God to continue working on my behalf, I must adhere to His statutes and remain humble before Him. Any area of darkness in the life of a believer is open to accusation by the enemy. When we walk in darkness in some areas, even if we do not realize what those areas are, satan has the right to attack us and accuse us before God. When this happens to us, we must quickly come into agreement with God's Word and repent over anything we may have done which could have subjected us to enemy attack.

Through this experience and others, God has truly enabled me to look past the faults of others but to be cautious concerning my heart and how their actions affect me. He has enabled me to see myself the way He sees me and I continue to trust Him to bring me into that perfect place of maturity in Him where peace and joy prevail. I am moving into a place of completeness although I am in the rebuilding process. To Him be glory and majesty forever. Amen.

"Walk in love, as Christ also has loved us and given Himself for us, an offering and a sacrifice to God for a sweet-smelling aroma."
—Ephesians 5:2

❦ *Chapter 9* ❦

HOW DID I GET HERE?

T his chapter was added just before publishing because God showed me something that I had not realized before. I have been praying for emotional healing in many areas of my life and what I had not realized is that for every relationship I have entered into, I searched for unconditional acceptance and love. I began to explore my childhood to discover why I constantly seek attention and affection, constantly desire affirmation and validation and why I have chosen the wrong companions for years.

What I came to realize is that although my father was and is a great provider, he is a good man; he has been deficient in expressing affection and love. I rarely remember receiving hugs or validation on achievements. I have searched all these years for the thing that I did not receive from my dad and that was for him to express that he loved me as his daughter. I do not have a recollection of seeing him openly show that he loved his kids any other way except discipline and being a good provider.

My mother hugged me and told me she loved me, she encouraged me when I was down, she was a nurturer. My dad was stern and firm. The overall perception was that he loved his children and his family; he just did not know how to show it "openly." I do not fault him because he was taught by my grandparents, particularly my grandmother, not to be affectionate. My grandmother was strong, she raised fourteen kids and she held the household together yet she rarely showed affection to her kids and grandkids thus teaching them to hold back their emotions.

I had not known how deeply I was affected by the lack of hugs and display of love in my home until now. All these years I have longed for the very thing I did not receive from my dad and in my searching I have suffered so much heart ache and pain. Many days and nights I have cried because I wondered if something was really wrong with me because I truly desired to have a loving companion in addition to a strong companion. I wanted to be held and told that I was loved and needed, wanted and desired. I attribute this deep sense of longing to the lack of affirmation in my childhood. I was an over-achiever, constantly trying to do really well at something just so that I would receive the recognition or acknowledgement of great accomplishment. The only time I remember my dad showing me open affection was when I accepted Jesus Christ as Lord and Savior at twelve years old. I vividly remember him kissing me on my forehead that day in church. Other than that, I do not remember him expressing love as I thought a parent should.

I believe the reason I have made so many bad choices is because I did not glean the lessons of how to choose properly from my dad. I am not saying he did not try to teach me, I just believe that I may have missed the lessons because I was so concerned about acceptance. I wanted to be accepted by friends, family and loved ones. I have seen and heard so many hurtful things within my family that I internalized many of them and those negative things shaped my perspective.

In my later adult years, I began to learn that my acceptance comes from God. He is the author and finisher of my faith and he is the only one who can truly validate who I am. I am fearfully and wonderfully made in His image but for many years I was not aware of God's love towards me. I did not really believe that God loved me because I had made so many mistakes – mistakes that I thought were completely un-forgiveable because people told me that I was a failure since I had messed up so much.

I want to encourage you as the reader today to truly search your past and search your heart if you are holding onto things from your childhood or things that may have caused you to make some bad deci-sions in life. It is not too late for God to restore and heal you but first you must acknowledge the "things" that are hindering your ability to move forward in life. The place where healing begins is the place where you acknowledge those things that have been hidden or that you have forgotten which have been stumbling blocks to making sound decisions in your relationships and other areas of your life.

My family is a great family. We have suffered many challenges and will probably face more. We are not perfect. We do not love the way we ought to sometimes but when tragedy strikes or when we need to fellowship we come together and embrace one another.

Love begins with God and should be shared with those closest to us before we can share it with anyone else. If we do not love our family members how can we possibly love others? God calls us to minister in our homes first and the take that ministry abroad. Until we master the ability to show love to our families, our children, our parents, sisters and brothers, our biological families or extended families we cannot possibly expect that God will enable us to truly share love with some-one we do not know.

My healing has begun. I am not completely whole but I have ex-posed the things in my life that caused me to get entangled in bondage and be susceptible to satan's tricks and devices. No longer does the enemy have a hold on my mental state or any other aspect of my life because his ploy has been uncovered. His desire to destroy me through emotional and mental turmoil is nullified with God's Word which was spoken over me before I was born. I thank God for my father and mother, my siblings, my daughter and all members of my family. I thank Him for the friends, the true friends who have embraced me and loved me and helped to shape my values.

I have messed up so many times but no longer will I be captive to bad choices or guilt and shame that the enemy brings. Satan is so crafty because he tempts us with those things he knows we like or that appeal to our flesh but then once we fall prey to them he accuses us of the very things that he tempted us with in the first place. When he does this, we must know that we are still a child of God and that we can be restored. We cannot allow our sins and mistakes to fester and cause us to go into deeper isolation because when we do we become more depressed and oppressed. We cannot allow the enemy to win by leading us down a wrong path and keeping us there. God is so wonderful that even when we sin, He will judge our sin and He will urge us to repent and turn back to Him.

Even though we may experience severe repercussions based on the nature of our sin or our weaknesses, He is still there to comfort us and strengthen us so that we do not lose heart. A loving Father chastens His children and when we need correction, God will provide it but He also shows us unconditional acceptance and love. He is the only one who truly loves us regardless of what we do. So how did I get here? I strayed from the path that God had for me but He loves me so much that He helped me to get back on the path through the prayers of the righteous and His Word. Jesus paid the price for all of our sins, He accepted me when He died on Calvary so whether my father openly expressed love or affirmation no longer matters because God's love covers a multitude of faults and discrepancies. I realize that my earthly father loves me and my heavenly Father loves me more. His love covers all sin and through Him I am redeemed. Through Jesus I am validated so I do not need assurance from man concerning who I am yet because of how God created me, I desire to experience His love from the hearts of those I love, particularly to experience true love from a man that He has chosen for me. No person should have to go through the things I have gone through. No man or woman should ever have to suffer from abuse just to be with another person because God did not create His children to be disrespected or abused.

When you suffer from emotional issues and depression people tend to label you and treat you as if you are different or "crazy." Many people in the Body of Christ are incapable of ministering to those who suffer from mental illness, low self-esteem or other issues related to emotional instability. A person who suffers from these conditions is often isolated and cast aside as being an "attention junky" or someone who is less than desirable to be around. My prayer is that Christians will become more attentive to the needs of those who require help in resolving emotional or mental issues and treat them as serious conditions that require intervention rather than neglect these individuals thus isolating them further.

"I make known the end from the beginning,
from ancient times, what is still to come. I say:
My purpose will stand, and I will do all that I please."
—Isaiah 46:10

❧ *Chapter 10* ❧

THE CONCLUSION
OF THE WHOLE MATTER

My prayer is that you have been blessed by the testimony set forth in this book. Although, I realize my words may not be all inclusive or may not be a complete cure for the relationship challenges many of us tend to face, it is a proclamation of my journey with God and the decisions that I have made which have led to much of the chastening He has given me with His mighty hand of love.

I purposely did not disclose specific details of circumstances that occurred because I did not want to deter you from the main purpose of this book which is ministry and encouragement to make better choices than I have made. The intent of my writing is never to disparage anyone or maliciously destroy anyone's life no matter what harm has been done to me.

God in His infamous wisdom knew that I would endure the trials and tribulations I have faced. He also knew that I would make every choice that I have made. He knows everything about me and He knew that I would be successful in some areas of my life and require more of His assistance in most. I love Him for who He is and for what He has done and will continue to do for me. His unconditional love and never ending mercy keep me in reverence to Him. I could not be who I am without Him and certainly He placed me within the right family, within right circle of friends; given me enemies and circumstances to mold me into a woman after His own heart and has placed me within the right church to learn, develop and grow into the woman of God He desires me to be.

I know that I gave my best in my marriage. I know that I made every effort to make it work and I glorified God through the midst of it all. My past experiences in other relationships taught me the value of investing in people and looking past my own selfish needs. I know that I loved my husband with my heart and I intently invested my best into our relationship. I always sought to please God first and as I did I was able to operate in a spirit of meekness for the majority of the time we were in covenant.

I thank God for the experience and time we shared because had I not gone through this traumatic experience I would not be able to truly speak candidly about emotional abuse. I do regret that I retaliated in anger against some of the things that occurred in my marriage and I regret that I did not remain in prayer; however, I am much stronger as a result of everything that has happened and I know exactly how to respond in the event I am faced with this type of situation again.

Throughout this season, I have prayed and given the situation to God yet things continued to escalate beyond my ability to maintain control and discretion. While I cannot change my actions I have learned from them immensely and I know that I will be especially cautious for future situations. I trust God to continue restoring unto to me the joy of His salvation and leading me by His Holy Spirit into truth and reconciliation by His Word.

Mr. Ancrum provided his time and energy to help a hurting soul such as myself. He gave me advice and wisdom, told me to keep God first and advised me to remain in quietness and stillness, waiting patiently for God's salvation; though I became distracted a few times, often slipping back into despondency and depression, I regained focus and I have completed what God has given me through this book. Again this is a work in progress, I am daily being healed and moving into a position of stability but it has taken a lot of time, work, energy and prayer to even get to the place where I can finally see some peace in my life.

What began as simple ministry to stabilize my life culminated into a project that I know only God could initiate. Without Deacon Ancrum's constant instruction to remain steadfast, despite what others thought or said about me, I may not have been here to see the vision God had given me come to pass. I suffered numerous days of isolation, loneliness, despair, illness, depression, weight loss and hair loss as a result of some of the choices I have made but God is still God and He can do anything but fail.

My deacon and his wife were available to minister to me at a time when my life seemed to be falling apart and he took the word of God, broke it and blessed it for me and I was inspired to begin writing again. Birthed from his availability to teach me this book was culminated. Although I had written many aspects of the book, it was not complete and Mr. Ancrum's teaching gave me the courage I needed to bring this book together. I thank God for Deacon Mike and his wife Elizabeth because they are truly people after God's own heart. Although not perfect, they exemplify the true meaning of Christian love. His teachings are profound and encouraging and every conversation with him begins and ends with God's Word. Simple life lessons with God's revelation are now brought to life upon these pages.

As I look back over the last two years of my life, I realize the assignment satan executed to destroy my marriage, my life and my effectiveness in God. He thought he had won but he has lost because this work is still being completed and God is healing me and beginning to use me again to do that which He has called me to do.

There were so many people brought into my marriage that should not have been and only my husband and I are to blame for that. The enemy sowed tares among the wheat God had planted. My husband and I never had an opportunity to love one another and we did not spend enough time with each other to appreciate the gifts we both offer.

Many people assumed I was a psychopathic wife who had no control over her emotions and actions. It "seemed" I was mentally disturbed because of how things were presented in public. Deeply hurting inside and outwardly portrayed as a woman who was insane, I could not disprove accusations because it clearly looked like I was unstable and incapable of functioning as a normal human being. Before I realized it, I was accused of being a lesbian, being bi-polar, being a gold-digger and a manipulator and none of those things were true.

People did not see the tearing and pulling I went through behind the scenes. They did not hear the arguments and fights over trivial matters. They did not hear the harsh verbal abuse and constant emotional suffering I endured. They did not see me sinking into depression because my self-esteem had plummeted. They did not see me crying night after night, day after day, week after week. They did not see the constant disrespect and alienation of affection, and the verbal threats before Sunday worship. And honestly I do not think many cared or wanted to see it. I was left to handle this with God because after all I had made my bed so I had to lie in it. People did not see the glimmers of hope that were given and they just did not understand what I went through as a woman who truly stood by her vow of marriage. The only option was to trust God and go back to a place of quietness so that He could heal my brokenness and restore me. The promises in His Word that He would fight for me are true and I know that the battle is truly His. God protected me over and over again; many times I just kept my mouth shut and I never spoke about any of the things that were going on. I had prayed so much that I thought God was tired of hearing my mouth but God heard and honored every single prayer because He opened a door for me to walk through so that I would no longer have to endure the pain.

As I begin to lift my voice in song again in praise and adoration, as I proclaim the truth of His Word and as I share the gifts He has placed within me, I know that He is able to make all grace abound toward me. God is so good and merciful, so kind and loving and His mercies are new every morning. He is so awesome to give us second chances. How can we not love Him and praise Him for just being God? God loves even me, a sinner saved by grace. He loves me a woman who is after His heart, a woman who has endured abuse, traumatic childhood experiences and seriously bad decisions regarding relationships.

You may find that much of the information I have shared with you from chapter to chapter sounds repetitive but I wanted to give you a clear picture of the things I dealt with during each stage of this cycle I put myself through. At each juncture I would progress and digress because I allowed the enemy to play upon my emotions and my heart. I allowed myself to become a victim to someone else's selfish desires and in so doing I kept going through the process over and over again until I shut down completely. The major points I want you as the reader to grasp are that emotional stability, wholeness, peace, joy and a solid foundation in Christ are necessary for any relationship in our lives to be healthy. As believers, every relationship we begin should begin with Christ and if we allow Him to be first we will always finish first. Moreover a solid relationship in Christ is important whether we have good days, bad days, disappointments or triumphs. No matter what comes or goes, our peace in God should remain and our joy should not be lost.

In your choices today, I pray that you will put God first, not just in your marriages and relationships but in everything you do. I pray that nothing shall be able to separate you from His love as Paul states in Romans 8:35-39. For He so loved us that He sent His only begotten Son; that we might not perish but have life eternal, that is why I praise Him and give Him all glory due His name.

Pray this prayer with me today if you need restoration or if you need salvation, "Father, forgive me for not loving you with my whole heart. Forgive me for not putting you first in my decisions and my heart. I realize today that I truly need you in my life and I cannot make it without you. Come into my life today, save me now and use me for your glory and honor. Mold me and shape me into the image of your dear Son Jesus who gave His life for me that I might live. I recognize that He died, He was buried and He rose again and has all power in His hands. Therefore, I commit my life to you, In Jesus Name, Amen."

"You are Holy, Oh so Holy. You are Holy, Oh so Holy. What a privilege and an honor to worship at Your throne, to be called into Your Presence as Your own. You are worthy, Oh so worthy. You are worthy, Oh so worthy, what a privilege and an honor to worship at Your throne, to be called into Your Presence as Your own. You are faithful, Oh so faithful. You are faithful, Oh so faithful. What a privilege and an honor to worship at Your throne, to be called into Your Presence as Your own... ."

—Lisa McClendon

SOURCES OF INSPIRATION

THE HOLY BIBLE (Nelson Study Bible NKJV and the Women of Faith Devotional Bible NI, KJV)

THE FIVE LOVE LANGUAGES by GARY CHAPMAN

THE PRAYER OF JABEZ by BRUCE WILKINSON

MANAGING YOUR EMOTIONS by JOYCE MEYER

BATTLEFIELD OF THE MIND by JOYCE MEYER

THE PURPOSE DRIVEN LIFE by RICK WARREN

SECRETS OF AN IRRESISTIBLE WOMAN by MICHELLE MCKINNEY-HAMMOND

HOW TO HEAR FROM GOD: Learn to Know His Voice and Make Right Decisions by JOYCE MEYER

ABOUT THE CONTRIBUTOR

MICHAEL J. ANCRUM was born in Greensboro, North Carolina and has been a resident of the Gate City for the majority of his life. He attended high school at Benjamin L. Smith. He is a singer, songwriter, and praise and worship leader at Love and Faith Christian Fellowship Church where he currently serves as an Administrative Deacon. Mr. Ancrum answered the call into ministry in 1990 and served as a minister under the leadership of Pastor Emanuel White at New Life Church of God in Christ located in Greensboro. He operates a local thrift store and owns Greater Greensboro Boxing Academy where he spends time encouraging and presenting the knowledge of Christ to the community and to young men and women. His e-book, a book for business and boxing, was released in October 2010. He utilizes his skills as a boxer and retired soldier to help teach discipline, restraint and purpose to males, particularly young African-American males who have found themselves in disadvantaged circumstances.

Mr. Ancrum is a mentor and teacher of God's Word and proclaims God's love in everything he does. He shares this life with his lovely wife Elizabeth, as they work in ministry together. He is the father of three children, LaPrecia Ancrum, Marquita Ancrum, and Michael Jr. He also has seven beautiful grandchildren, Dwaycia, Armani, Christopher, Josiah, Avian, King and Brooklyn.

Along with Ms. Barrino, Mr. Ancrum has dispelled the works of the enemy, helped to destabilize the works of the flesh and iniquity that have presented themselves during this season of God's work and fought to bring forth God's glory by offering to Him the sacrifice of praise and thanksgiving during a time when hope seemed to be lost. His efforts and contributions to this work are innumerable and he is immensely appreciated for his prayers and devotion to accomplishing the will of God through this endeavor.

Much time was spent pulling this project together and it would not have come to full fruition without the ministry support that "Brother Mike" gave to Ms. Barrino. Through many tears and a lot of prayer the vision that God has birthed within each of them has come to pass.

ABOUT THE AUTHOR

ANGEL BARRINO is the CEO and owner of Angel B. Enterprises LLC, the parent company for several businesses providing health, spiritual and marketing strategies. She is an International BEST selling author; a lover of God and people. A multifaceted entrepreneur, she began her journey as a young girl selling Girl Scout cookies, candy bars and other items. She believes in and breathes entrepreneurship. Angel is an avid writer, psalmist, and speaker using her gifts to inspire others on a daily basis. In 2010 she founded Purpose and Praise Ministries which focuses on bringing restoration to broken lives. Additionally, she is the owner of The Praise Network Greensboro, a full media broadcasting site which encompasses radio and television.

Ms. Barrino is a former inspirational writer for *The PUSH Report*, *Simply Elevate Magazine*, *Huami Magazine*, and *Anointed Fire Online Magazine*. She has been featured in *Simply Elevate Magazine* (August 2013); *The PUSH Report*, *Huami Magazine*, *Greensboro Live Magazine* and *The BWE Online Journal*. She has appeared on *The Sharvette Mitchell Show*, *This Needs to be Said* with Katherine Waddell, *Walking in Power* with BJ Relefourd, *The Anthony and B Fly Show* and other radio shows with Richelle Tamu Shaw, Cason Bolton and countless others. She has worked with numerous authors and writers, helping create several BEST selling authors since her company was incepted. She coaches authors virtually and in person to help them bring their book projects to life from beginning to end. Her company specializes in supporting authors at any stage of the process.

She is the author of *Becoming One Flesh: Marriage God's Way* and the co-creator of the newly released book *Organized Obstacles: An Underdog Anthology*, www.organizedobstacles.com, organizedobstacles@gmail.com

Ms. Barrino has gained new strength and insight on what the Father really requires to maintain a healthy God centered marriage or relationship. After her second marriage to the father of American Idol winner Fantasia Barrino; Angel began focusing on building and restoring relationships in all aspects of her life while ministering to those who experience similar situations. She has been given a ministerial vision that compels believers to learn the principles behind holding a marriage together and choosing mates based on biblical principles. The primary focus is spiritual, emotional and mental compatibility. She strongly believes a mate, who possesses these characteristics is the perfect will of the Father. Through fervent prayer, she petitions on behalf of marriages worldwide; praying the enemy's stronghold on families and marriages will be broken. Strong marriages provide a more solid foundation for the Body of Christ to minister to a dying world. Additionally, she hopes to share her life with someone in a beautiful, God focused marriage. She teaches the principle that strong families and marriages, build strong ministries and churches, which leads to strong communities. She has an adamant love for members of impoverished society yet possesses the ability to minister to people from all walks of life. Having a heart for those who severely suffer from depression, emotional and mental illness including low self-esteem; she offers assistance and coaching to those who desire it.

She is an advocate for Domestic Violence Prevention and Awareness; using her experiences and those of others to encourage women, men and children to remove themselves from harmful and abusive relationships. She has partnered with several women and agencies within the community to help bring awareness to this growing plague affecting all communities nationwide and globally.

In January 2010, she was diagnosed with Lupus, a serious autoimmune disease which affected her health greatly. As a result of this diagnosis, she began a journey of wellness through Herbalife International and received her certification as a personal wellness coach in 2011. She adamantly attributes her health testimony to God and these phenomenal products. In December 2012, she opened her own nutrition club, Inspired Nutrition Station and later transitioned her business to virtual coaching and online support.

Angel is a member of Tabernacle of Meeting under the leadership of Pastor Russell Miller. She is a native of Greensboro, NC and travels often, supporting others with their endeavors. Her beautiful daughter Janae, has been the source of much of her success, motivation and inspiration. Ms. Barrino cherishes family, friends and mentors, attributing their 'teaching' as a significant part of her success as well.

Through her platform she wholeheartedly supports entrepreneurs, independent authors and gospel artists, helping them gain exposure and enhance their projects. Among her other achievements, she has participated in the recording of two albums; one of which she was a lead vocal on the song "The Storm" written by Dionn Owens the director and producer for The Renaissance Community Choir based our of Winston-Salem, NC. She is a former member of the gospel group The Promise, under the direction and expertise of Jeffrey Adams, Washington, D.C. In her spare time she enjoys walking, designing jewelry and spending time with loved ones.

FROM THE HEART
OF THE AUTHOR:

So much went into the creating of this book; Time and energy, thought and prayer, revisions, proofreading, editing, promoting, distribution and marketing. Yet even with all of that none of it matters if God had not put His hand upon it. I am just a vessel, poured out and emptied from life's circumstances and this endeavor brought so much healing into my life and so much to the forefront for me that God dealt with and He has taught me so many lessons just through the mirror image of His Word as reflected in these pages. I pray that you have been blessed and will continue to be blessed. With each new day, I thank God for the foundation and well-rounded life He has given me, the family He placed me in and at each stage of my spiritual growth the people He has allowed to come into my life either for good or bad. I have been favored with His love and grace, His mercy and protection; therefore, I am truly grateful.

All the Best,

Angel B.

BONUS CHAPTER
THE RECAP

Purpose in the Pain, Healing through the Aftermath

When I thought about what I would share in this chapter, I remembered the words of a dear friend which were, "this book is not for all but it is for some and it will cross barriers." My friends, it has crossed barriers and boundaries; it has crossed ethnicities and cultures; cities, states and countries. For that I am eternally grateful. I remember thinking about writing a sequel of all of the subsequent events that occurred; I remember asking myself, "should I tell this or should I tell that?" My mind was plagued with all sorts of thoughts in 2010. I made some huge mistakes. My ex-husband made some huge mistakes. We hurt each other. Other people were hurt in the process. Many days I lived in regret over my decisions. There was so much pain that I never thought it would end. The light at the end of the tunnel seemed like a distant mirage or non-existent. People wondered if we'd take each other back. Initially I believe both of us wanted reconciliation – but the pain . . . oh it was so great. Who could possibly overcome this magnitude of damage? Certainly I could not, but if God said so I was willing to repair the breach. Albeit I risked losing friendships and family member relationships but for the cause of God's will, if it were His will for my husband and I to reconcile, I was willing to take the chance.

One lonely night, as I prayed and meditated upon which direction to take I remember the Holy Spirit whispering, "It's your choice." Each time I prayed for reconciliation to occur, my husband and I only argued. The conversations would start out beautiful but by the time they ended we were yelling at one another. That had to stop and it did. I stopped taking the calls, I changed my phone number, and I stopped answering the past. The tearing and destruction had to end – and I ended it. The Holy Spirit also reminded me that the associated sins and darkness we both lived in were forgiven and washed away. People would remember, as they always do, of course; but my "daddy," my Abba Father had released them and remembered them no more. This is the act of love and reconciliation, the power of forgiveness if you will that Yahuwah extends to His beloved children. His mercy and grace covers all things. If you belong to Him, "it is Finished!"

Although still married to Mr. Barrino, I was "okay" with being apart. He had filed for a divorce in 2010 which was immediately dismissed (this process of separation continued until October 2014). Initially, I was angry that I was still married to him but yet a part of me was relieved. Deep down a part of me really wanted this thing to turn around but on the surface I cried and I was angry because I was still attached to this person who seemed to hate me so much. I cried in the court room when the judge said, "I'm sorry Ms. Barrino. The paperwork is too procedurally incorrect and I cannot grant your divorce." I was angry because he blamed me that the divorce did not go through. I was angry because God was not fixing my situation but I saw Him fix other broken marriages. A flood of feelings overwhelmed me as I walked out the court room feeling defeated that day. I felt myself going through darkness yet again. I was tired, I was drained. When God says in His Word that He hates divorce it is because He did not design marriage to end. Marriage, Godly marriage is the closest relationship on earth that resembles a believer's relationship with Him. To end a marriage is truly like a death because intimacy creates a bond that is very difficult to break. I had a soul tie with my husband that was not easily broken, although the incidences that occurred during our marriage ended our union. I still thought of him nearly every day for almost two years – even though I tried desperately to forget everything associated with him. The thoughts would not go away which yielded me to more anguish and despair. The roller coaster had to end. Whoever said the quickest way to get over one man is to find another one was obviously insane to some degree because I attempted this illogical act of coping and medicating; needless to say it failed. God was not pleased and I was miserable. Quickly repenting of my actions, I began my journey again of healing and restoration – all the while still married to this man.

People asked, "Why are you still married to him?" Friends and family wondered why I seemed to still hang on. But I wasn't hanging on as much as I was growing through the process. I did not want the divorce. He did. Therefore, I did not feel as if I should be the one to file for the divorce. But eventually I made a decision that if he did not file I was going to because my life was hindered in every area by this tie that I had with someone who did not love me.

One day I relinquished my desire to tell the ugly story to the entire world, the tabloids, and Oprah. I don't really know when that took place but I know when it did I was healed completely. The aftermath was great, but my healing was greater. Yes, back then I wanted the world to know. But at what cost? Five years ago I went through all the stages of grief. There was shock, disbelief, low self-esteem, blaming, anger, disappointment, sadness, grieving, acceptance, and more grieving. But then one day everything changed and joy filled my heart. I had forgiven myself. I had forgiven him and I had forgiven others. This entire process took about 3.5 years but it happened. Darkness soon changed to light. The spirit of heaviness lifted and a garment of praise and worship emerged. No longer was I bound by 'evil forebodings' and feelings of inadequacy or guilt. I was a new creature, made in the image of my almighty Father and His precious Son. Forgiveness, restoration and reconciliation do not necessarily mean you and the individual will re-unite as a couple. Sometimes it just means you will be able to move forward without bitterness, shame and regret. We both moved forward. And now my life is in a divine place. My purpose became so clear through this process. One of the most profound revelations I teach people, which is also a central theme of this book, is that God's process is to tear down, destroy and rebuild. The first few chapters of this book reveal my tearing down and destruction process – not physically but spiritually. Those things God could not use in the Kingdom were removed and replaced by those things He can use. The last few chapters, including this one, reveal my rebuilding process. As I look back over these last several years I am amazed at what I walked through to get to this place where I am now. Freedom has a whole new meaning for me. Facing the day means something different. Embracing and cherishing each moment are rules I live by. My life has a new direction, my perspective has changed. My stress level has been reduced. My purpose has been birthed and my divine destiny being revealed daily. My Abba Father knew the plans He had for me, plans to prosper me and not to harm me, to give me an expected end (Jeremiah 29:11).

"How precious are His thoughts towards me, how great is the number of things He thinks toward me (Psalm 139:17)." Who would have known that out of this pain would be written one of the greatest healing tools for restoration and forgiveness? Who would have known that out of this pain would be birthed my businesses and freedom to help others daily? Who would have known that out of this glitch in my life, this season of interruption and misdirection would come purpose and destiny causing my life to be catapulted into full-time ministry, business and greatness? This thing that hurt me helped me; it was designed to kill me but my God used it to save my life and restore me. How can I not serve Him? How can I not love Him? Or trust Him? He has proven His love for me more than I can imagine. For this I give Him praise.

OTHER ACKNOWLEDGEMENTS:

◆ **To Bishop Sheldon McCarter & Co-Pastor Joyce McCarter:**
You imparted so much into my life, thank you for teaching me so much and blessing me with God's Word.

◆ **To Pastor Reginald Holiday & First Lady Holiday:**
Thank you for the season I served in your ministry, I learned so much and I am so grateful for your humble spirits and teaching.

◆ **To Pastor Larry Fitzgerald & First Lady Fitzgerald:**
Pastor Larry & First Lady Fitzgerald, my spirit grew by leaps and bounds under your leadership, you nurtured me and my family, was there to visit when we were sick, you baptized my daughter and you never turned a deaf ear. You are the epitome of true servants of Christ. Thank you.

Last but never least to all of the people who have sown into this ministry and into my life, thank you so much; to my BFFs for life – Angela Mahoney and Latishia Mitchener and my "nephew" Jacob – I love you from the bottom of my heart – through all of my trials, my good, bad and ugly you have been there – THANK YOU!

I especially want to thank Ms. Betty Benton, Danielle Gilmer - my Public Relations Representative, Lawana Best - my administrative assistant, Tammy Ingram, Nataisha Pointzes and Created to Conquer Ministries, Created to Care Prayer Ministry, Treasured Vessels International, The Sons of Zion, and all of the countless other family and friends for being so supportive and encouraging; you are and have been a tremendous blessing to Purpose and Praise Ministries. Love you and thank you so much!

– A. Barrino

CONTACT INFORMATION:

Purpose and Praise Ministries

Websites: www.angelbarrino.com
www.indieauthorsandmore.biz
Phone: (704) 978-8679
Email: angelbinspired@gmail.com
PRAISE@sibn.net
Estore: www.createspace.com/3485060

Please visit The Praise Network for inspirational music,
business information, upcoming book releases and more.
Prayer requests can be sent to purposeandpraise@gmail.com

Follow Ms. Barrino on Facebook at:
www.facebook.com/hpmp.angelb or www.facebook.com/abarrino
Follow on Twitter at: @angelBinspired or
www.twitter.com/praise_network

Mr. Ancrum can be contacted via email at:
mike.ancrum@yahoo.com

Organized Obstacles site information:
www.organizedobstacles.com, organizedobstacles@gmail.com

Made in the USA
Middletown, DE
08 September 2023

37705497R00086